JOHN WESLEY
ON
THE GREAT SALVATION

I + m L

Herbert Boyd Mcgonigle

MA, BD, DD, PHD

Former Lecturer at Nazarene Theological College, Dene Road,
Didsbury, Manchester, in the classes in Church History, Theology
and Wesley Studies, Former Principal of Nazarene Theological
College and now Principal Emeritus

British Library Cataloguing in Publication Data.
A catalogue record for this book is available from the British Library

ISBN 978 0 86071 729 4

A commissioned Publication

Printed by Moorleys Print & Publishing Ltd

MOORLEYS
PRINTERS

info@moorleys.co.uk / www.moorleys.co.uk

Preface

Dedicated to Jeanne

On Sunday, 5ᵗʰ of February, 2017, at a quarter past seven in the morning, my darling wife Jeanne entered the kingdom of heaven. She was taken to hospital at 4:30 on Saturday and the nurse found her dead at a quarter past seven. Doctors and nurses attended her during the night every half an hour and she slipped away peacefully in her sleep. Our sons, Stephen and Jonathan, and my step-son, Keith, accompanied me to the hospital and we said our farewell. We had been married for fifty-five years and five months and we loved each other every day of our lives! She travelled with me to Japan on two occasions, she went with me to America on three occasions, to Europe also, and she visited the churches where I was preaching close on forty years. She shared with me in the churches; in Walthamstow, in Uddingston near Glasgow, in Leeds, and now, fifty-five years and five months later, she was my greatest supporter. In 1978 I published my first book, William Cooke on Entire Sanctification, *she read it through and encouraged me to write more. She continued to read my books until I had published the twenty-fourth;* General William Booth, *and she promised to read more! That's the reason I am publishing this volume,* John Wesley on The Great Salvation, *and I am dedicating this to Jeanne.*

I am delighted that the Revd. Karl Stanfield, Th.B, M.A., has offered to write the Foreword. Karl was a student in the Nazarene Theological College, Manchester, 1981-1985, and I was his lecturer in Church History, Wesley Studies and Homiletics. For five years he has been our Pastor and Jeanne and I enjoyed going there every Sunday morning to a full Church. Karl comes from Lurgan and I come from Enniskillin and that can't be bad! In a lecture in Wesley Studies in 1984 I mentioned to the class that sometimes hymns are used to give an emphasis and I quoted one, written by Charles Wesley, that uses love to express how great the theme was to Charles Wesley:

> Was great to speak a world from nought
> Was greater to redeem!

Karl came to me and asked what was the hymn that I had mentioned. I told him I couldn't remember but I would go through the hymns and tell him what I had found. I had a collection of, Hymns For The Use Of The People Called Methodists, *a thousand and eight hymns, and I promised to go through them, reading thirty each night. It took me almost a month and then I found it; 950! Its opening lines were:*

>The Lord of Sabbath let us praise
>In concert with the blessed.

However, it wasn't one of the Wesleys who wrote it, but Samuel Wesley (1690-1739), the elder brother of John and Charles. I showed it to Karl and I've heard him repeat it on several occasions. I told Jeanne about it and that it had taken me a month to find it. Jeanne replied that if I had taken the Irish way, beginning at the end and reading back, I could have found it on the second night! Now that she has gone, I will miss her love and care for me for fifty-five years and five months.

FOREWORD

I first met the McGonigles when I started attending College (BINC, as it was called then) back in 1981. My first early morning class started at 7.50 and it was a Church History survey module with the Revd. Dr. Herbert Boyd McGonigle a lecturer. By the time that first class ended at 8.50am, my hand was sore writing! It was the first of many classes I sat under Dr. McGonigle as my tutor. I also recall the college weekends, taking church services in various places in a locality. Needless to say, in those days, it comprised of a Saturday evening rally with two services on Sunday. On the way home in Dr. McGonigle's Austin Cambridge we played word games as we travelled along.

I remember well the hospitality enjoyed with both Herbert and Jeanne when they would invite students home for Sunday lunch and after we would play on their six-foot snooker table; happy days. Needless to say, their love of all things Wesleyan shone through; from music to theology, ceramics and the history of the Wesley family. This continues strongly even through until today. Dr. McGonigle still rises early at 6.00am to read and enjoy writing. Now in this edition, his 25th short book on the work and influence of the Wesleys, we have a very special publication written by Herbert and dedicated to the memory of his wife and companion of over fifty-five years.

The support of friends from years gone by, the prayers of his local Nazarene Church at Brooklands and the District, plus the ever present help and care shown by the family must certainly be a great source of comfort and solace at this time of personal loss. I gladly commend this very special edition in this ongoing series to everyone! As with all the previous books, it is thorough and thoughtful and inspirational; we would expect nothing less. Twice in a recent sermon, I did quote from the chapter, *John Wesley: The Supremacy of Grace.*

Personally, I have very much appreciated my happy years at college, albeit now a generation ago. The Revd. Dr. H. McGonigle was my Church History, Wesley Studies and Homiletics teacher. Today he is a member of my church and I am his pastor. It's all been a privilege really; especially being asked to write the Foreword on this occasion. I hope, like me, you enjoy and are enriched by this exceptional work.

With appreciation,
Revd. Karl Stanfield
22nd February 2017

JOHN WESLEY: THE SUPREMACY OF GRACE

The year 1725 was an important one in John Wesley's life, both in terms of its own immediate significance and its repercussions on his eventual ministry. In that year he graduated from Christ Church and on 19 September, he was ordained deacon by Bishop Potter. It was in preparation for ordination that Wesley began to enquire deeply into the relationship between divine providence and human responsibility, a question that would engage his attention for the rest of his life. His ordination vow included his expressed acceptance of the Church of England's *Thirty-Nine Articles*, and he hesitated over the wording of Article XVII. Entitled 'Of Predestination and Election,' it declared:

> Predestination to Life is the everlasting purpose of God, whereby (before the foundations of the world were laid) he hath constantly decreed by his counsel secret to us, to deliver from curse and damnation those whom he hath chosen in Christ out of mankind, and to bring them by Christ to everlasting salvation, as vessels made to honour.[1]

In correspondence with his mother Susanna on this Article, she offered an interpretation based on an understanding of God's foreknowledge; viz. God predestined those whom he foresaw would respond in obedience to the invitation of the gospel. John was convinced that this interpretation allowed him to swear his allegiance to the Article and fifty years later he republished his mother's letter on the subject, evidence that his subscription was a life-long conviction.

Alongside this consideration of how the doctrines of predestination and human responsibility can be reconciled, ran Wesley's growing interest in human sinfulness and how God's grace works for man's salvation. Studies in John Wesley's life and doctrines written in the 19th and early 20th centuries tended to pay very little attention to his writings and publications prior to May, 1738. That year marked the evangelical turning point in his life and such was the concentration of attention on the Aldersgate 'heart-warming,' that his doctrinal

---

[1]   Article XVII, 1719, p.302.

emphases prior to that year tended to be given less attention. Yet in the years from 1725 until 1738 John Wesley was developing his understanding of mankind created in the image of God and he evolved a doctrine of universal sinfulness that became foundational for all his later anthropology and soteriology.

His very first sermon, preached two weeks after his ordination, dealt with how death removes the Christian from present miseries into the bliss of everlasting life. Death frees us from the tyranny of sin and the 'seeds of corruption were so deeply implanted.'[2] Similar sentiments are expressed in sermons preached in the following five years but it is in the first 'university sermon' that the issues of sin and grace come to the fore. In November 1730 Wesley preached in St Mary's, Oxford, and his theme was the *imago Dei*, mankind made in the divine image, how that image was marred in the Fall and the hope of its restoration by Christ's redemption. Wesley postulated that the characteristic of unfallen Adam was that love 'filled the whole expansion of his soul…. Every movement of his heart was love.'[3] This is an important emphasis to note in John Wesley's first Oxford sermon, because for the greater part of his ministry he would insist that the possibility of salvation from all sin in this life is in terms of love perfected. In its main points, however, the sermon fell far short of Wesley's later doctrines of grace. It proclaimed that the Holy Spirit enables the Christian to exercise humility and charity and this is the way of salvation. There is little emphasis on Christ's atonement for sin and none at all on justification, regeneration and new birth.

At this time Wesley was deeply exercised over the question of original sin, the freedom of the will and the operation of God's grace. In the month following his ordination in 1725 he had read Humphrey Ditton's essay on the origin of evil and in 1729 he read it again. In a letter to his father in December that year he outlined Ditton's main

---

[2]   *The Bicentennial Edition of the Works of John Wesley*, Edited by Frank Baker: 20 volumes; Oxford: Clarendon Press/Nashville, TN: Abingdon Press, 1975-95, Vol. 4, p.212. Hereafter cited as J. Wesley, *Works [BE]*.
[3]   J. Wesley, *Works [BE]*, Vol. 4, p.294.

arguments who spoke of the 'mighty question' of *unde malum*, 'whence came evil?' Ditton's conclusion, with which Wesley is in general agreement, is that the Biblical account points to the wrong use of our liberty, a possibility inevitable given the finiteness of a created nature.

> But the plain truth is, the hypothesis requires no more to the confutation of it than the bare proposing it. Two supreme, independent principles is next door to a contradiction in terms. It is the very same thing, in result and consequence, as saying two absolute infinities; and he that says two, had as good say ten or fifty, or any other number whatever. Nay, if there can be two essentially, distinct, absolute infinities, there may be an infinity of such absolute infinities; that is as much as to say, none of them all would be an absolute infinite; or that none of them all would be properly and really infinite.[4]

In another letter to his father a year later he reported that he had recently read Archbishop King's 'celebrated treatise' on original sin but found it the least convincing of all the works he had read on that subject. King, he alleged, was resurrecting the old Stoic heresy of the necessary evil of matter. A month later he sent his father a very full outline of King's book in which he summarised it somewhat differently from his earlier evaluation. Now, he argues, that freedom of choice is consistent with the Creator's purpose and that the possibility of falling into sin could only have been prevented either by God removing all possibilities of temptation or always constraining in his creatures to choose what is good, but both these providences would have denied the very liberty that God had chosen to bestow.

> The more of this power any being possesses, the less subject he is to the impulses of external agents and the more commodious is his condition. Happiness rises from a due use of our faculties: if, therefore, this be the noblest of all our faculties, then our chief happiness lies in the due use of this - that is, in our elections.... and into these foolish choices we may be betrayed either by ignorance, negligence, by indulging the exercise of liberty too far, by obstinacy or habit, or lastly, by the importunity of our natural appetites. Hence

---

[4] J. Wesley, *The Letters of the Rev. John Wesley*, 1931, Vol. 1, p.45. Hereafter cited as J. Wesley, *Letters*.

it appears how cautious we ought to be in choosing; for though we may alter our choice, yet to make that alteration is painful - the more painful the longer we have persisted in it.[5]

In March 1730 John Wesley read Richard Lucas', *An Enquiry after Happiness*, a book that Susanna Wesley had read carefully and approved very highly. Lucas was primarily concerned about the relationship between happiness and holiness and argued for a deliverance from sin in this life, an argument in which he defined sin in terms of the deliberate transgression of God's law. The following year, in reply to a question put to him on the nature of sin, Wesley replied, almost in Lucas' exact words, that sin is 'a voluntary breach of a known law.'[6] A few months later he repeated this definition of sin to another enquirer.[7] It is clear that from 1729 onwards John Wesley was increasingly pre-occupied with questions about the origins of sin, the nature and extent of human freedom and the means whereby God's saving grace works for the salvation of fallen humanity.

It was, however, in his 1733 Oxford sermon, *The Circumcision of the Heart*, that John Wesley laid out the fullest exposition of his understanding of sin, grace and holiness that he had yet enunciated. There is no Enlightenment optimism here about the innate goodness of human beings.

> We are by nature 'wretched, and poor, and miserable, and blind, and naked.' It convinces that in our best estate we are of ourselves all sin and vanity; that confusion, and ignorance, and error, reign over our understanding; that unreasonable, early, sensual, devilish passions usurp authority over our will: in a word, there is no whole part in our soul, that all the foundations of our nature are out of course.[8]

By 'the circumcision of the heart' Wesley explained that he means being cleansed from inner sin, being endued with the virtues of Christ and being so renewed in mind as to be perfect even 'as our Father in

---

[5] J. Wesley, *Letters*, Vol. 1, pp.71, 72.
[6] J. Wesley, *Letters*, Vol. 1, p.91.
[7] J. Wesley, *Letters*, Vol. 1, p.111.
[8] J. Wesley, *Works [BE]*, Vol. 1, p.403.

heaven is perfect.'[9] In summary it means cultivating the virtues of humility, faith, hope and love. In spite of the many Pauline quotations that Wesley employs, his understanding is far from being a Pauline understanding of salvation by faith. Instead the sermon breathes the atmosphere of 'Oxford Methodism,' and the influence of the writings of William Law is very apparent. In spite of the sound superstructure about universal sinfulness and the pervasiveness of moral evil, the sermon is an attempt to establish a doctrine of sanctification but without a basic understanding of justification. It is of the greatest significance that when John Wesley published this sermon fifteen years later, he added a paragraph to his original text. The paragraph spoke of 'a divine conviction of his free, unmerited love to me a sinner, a sure confidence in his pardoning mercy, wrought in us by the Holy Ghost – a confidence whereby every believer is enabled to bear witness that I have.... Redemption through his blood, even the forgiveness of sins.'[10] Albert Outler rightly comments that in 1733 John Wesley was still preoccupied with holy living but in 1748 he added 'his discovery of *justifying* faith as unmerited mercy and as the assurance of forgiveness through the merits of Christ's propitiatory death.'[11]

Shortly before he sailed for Savannah in October 1735, Wesley wrote a letter to Richard Morgan, a member of the Oxford 'Holy Club.' This was a reference to Dr. William Tilly, a high churchman who had published his *Sixteen Sermons* in 1712 and which Wesley had first read in 1732. As he did with many others writings he liked, Wesley made extracts from Tilly's sermons and preached from them on at least four occasions. Two of Tilly's sermons were entitled, 'The Grace of God shown to be Consistent with the Liberty of man's Will,' and were expositions of Philippians 2:12, 13. These were the sermons that Wesley commended so highly in 1735, presumably because he was in full agreement that the provisions and accomplishments of divine grace in man's salvation were in harmony with the exercise of human

---

[9]   Matthew 5:48.
[10]   J. Wesley, *Works [BE]*, Vol. 1, p.405.
[11]   J. Wesley, *Works [BE]*, Vol. 1, p.405, footnote.

self-determination. Tilly was well versed on the history of the grace and free-will dispute in Christian theology. He repudiated both the claims of the Pelagians whose emphasis on human ability diminished the sovereignty of grace, and the fatalism of those who so restricted human response that salvation for the elect was irresistible. In the unregenerate man the powers of the soul are 'exceedingly bruised and enfeebled' and this is the consequence of the Fall.

Tilly strongly urged that God is not under obligation to either accept or reward those good works done by unregenerate men. That such good works are done Tilly does not doubt, but echoing Article XIII he declares they are done out of vanity, pride and vainglory and not out of penitence and sorrow for sin. In this condition of bondage to sin God works preveniently by the grace of baptismal regeneration.

Tilly's argument here on 'preventing' or prevenient grace was a commonplace in Anglican theology and represented the teaching of Article X of the *Thirty-Nine Articles*. Entitled 'Of Free Will,' it spoke of mankind 'after the fall of Adam,' as having 'no power to do good works pleasant and acceptable to God, without the grace of God by Christ preventing us, that we may have a good will, and working with us, when we have that good will.'[12] When John Wesley wrote in 1735 of Tilly's sermons on free will as 'the best I ever saw,'[13] it was not their originality he was commending, rather the perspicacity with which Tilly's arguments were presented. Wesley was very well aware that this understanding of God's grace preceding all spiritual response in the sinner's heart had been widely and consistently taught in 16th and 17th century Anglican theology. While Wesley would not argue for the beginnings of prevenient grace in baptismal regeneration, as Tilly did, yet he later espoused a doctrine of prevenient grace that was markedly close to Tilly's. Both these Oxford dons attempted to hold, in a tension of soteriological balance, both the priority of God's awakening grace and the sinner's enabled ability to respond to that grace.

---

[12]   Article X, 1678, p.300.
[13]   J. Wesley, *Letters*, Vol. 1, p.184.

This survey of John Wesley's reading and preaching between 1725 and 1738 results in some important conclusions about his developing theological convictions. The whole question of the origin and pervasiveness of sin in human experience had early captured his thinking and would remain a lifelong interest. With a near-Augustinian understanding of the guilt and power of sin, Wesley was deeply committed to the Anglican emphasis on universal grace expressed in Article XXXI.[14] Whatever questions may be thrown up as to how and why and where God's grace works in fallen humanity, Wesley was convinced that a strict Genevan interpretation of predestination begged more questions than it answered. From his wide reading in the Fathers, the English Puritans, and especially the Anglican and high church theologians, Wesley evolved an *ordo salutis*, a 'way of salvation,' that stressed the priority of God's saving grace. What is particularly important to note is that the main elements of this *ordo* were in place by 1735. This was prior to his Aldersgate 'heart-warming,' prior even to his meeting the Moravians. That encounter would certainly have important repercussions on how Wesley subsequently understood and proclaimed both saving faith and the relationship between justification and sanctification. By 1735 John Wesley's *ordo salutis* was essentially soteriological. He was constructing a theology of grace that would answer, for himself and for those who heard him, the great question, What must I do to be saved?

With the commencement of Wesley's evangelistic ministry in Bristol in March 1739, there began also his half-century of writing and publishing in the interests of the work of the revival. As well as the scores of sermons and the hundreds of letters, there were extracts from the writings of others that Wesley believed were helpful in building faith and promoting holy living in the lives of his 'Methodist' people. His interest in all this publishing enterprise, which eventually numbered some four hundred items, was primarily practical and pastoral. 'I write chiefly for plain, unlettered men,' he claimed, 'who

---

[14] Article XXXI, 1678, 'The offering of Christ once made is that perfect redemption, propitiation, and satisfaction, for all the sins of the whole world, both original and actual, and there is none other satisfaction for sin, but that alone.'

understand only their mother tongue.... And have a desire to save their souls.'[15]   When he began to publish his fifty-volume *A Christian Library* in 1749, he subtitled it, *A Christian Library: Consisting of Extracts from and Abridgements of the Choicest Pieces of Practical Divinity.*[16] Wesley adjudged the position clearly.

> That the piety which has shone in many of our own countrymen, has been equal to their learning? They were indeed burning and shining lights, in their successive generations; men whom the Spirit of God endued with the truest wisdom, and taught to understand even the deep things of God.... I have made, as I was able, an attempt of this kind. I have endeavoured to extract such a collection of English Divinity, as (I believe) is all true, all agreeable to the oracles of God: as in all practical, unmixed with controversy of any kind; and all intelligible to plain men.... but going down to the depth, and describing the height of Christianity.... but all conspire together 'to make the man of God, thoroughly furnished unto every good word and work.'[17]

Very early in the work of the revival when divisions were appearing among the converts in Bristol on the questions of grace, free will and human responsibility, Wesley found a work by Isaac Watts that he believed answered the situation. Watts' tract argued that God not only sincerely offers salvation to all men, but he also provides a sufficiency of grace that accompanies the offer of salvation. While not using the term 'prevenient grace,' yet it is clear that this is what Watts had in mind. It is by the Spirit that sinners hear and recognise the gracious call of God and by that same Spirit they are prompted to seek after God. The gospel offers to them both the promise of forgiveness and the inner working of the Spirit in their hearts to persuade and empower them to respond. Here was a powerful apologia on both universal grace and the divine initiative in human response, from the pen of a respected Dissenter that allowed Wesley just what he needed in the current dispute. He was attempting to construct an *ordo salutis* that moved from what he called the first 'faint glimmering ray' of light, of spiritual awareness and alienation from God, right through the stages

---

[15]   J. Wesley, Preface, *Explanatory Notes upon The New Testament,* Vol. 2, 1754.
[16]   J. Wesley, *A Christian Library*, Vols. 1 to 50.
[17]   J. Wesley, Preface, *A Christian Library*, Vol. 1, pp.5-9.

of salvation to final glorification. Given his early proclivity to the study of the origins of evil and his concerns with how God's grace operates to cancel and conquer sin in human hearts, it is not surprising that his *ordo* laid a very firm foundation of universal sin and estrangement from God. While this can be illustrated from almost every sermon and theological tract that he published, an early sermon established a thesis from which he never departed. Entitled, *The Way to the Kingdom*, and first published in 1748, it represented Wesley's evangel since the beginnings of his itinerancy in Bristol. Having shown what the kingdom of God is, Wesley then declared that the way into that kingdom is by repentance. It was under this heading that he outlined his understanding of that original and actual sin that puts the entire world under condemnation.

> Know thyself to be a sinner, and what manner of sinner thou art. Know that corruption of thy inmost nature.... Know that thou art corrupted in every power, in every faculty of thy soul, that thou art totally corrupted in every one of these.... The eyes of thine understanding are darkened, so that they cannot discern God or the things of God.... Thy will is no longer the will of God, but is utterly perverse and distorted, averse from all good, from which God loves, and prone to all evil, to every abomination which God hateth. Thy affections are alienated from God, and scattered abroad over all the earth.... Such is the inbred corruption of thy heart, of thy very inmost nature.... From this evil fountain flow forth the bitter streams of vanity, thirst of praise, ambition, covetousness, the lust of the flesh, the lust of the eye, and the pride of life. From this arise anger, hatred, malice, revenge, envy, jealousy, evil surmisings.[18]

From this stark portrayal of human sinfulness and spiritual impotence, Wesley proceeded to spell out the consequences. The wages of sin is death, not only temporal but eternal death. The sinner deserves 'God's wrath and everlasting damnation.' Every sinner 'is under the sentence of hell-fire, doomed already, just dragging to destruction.' Of himself the sinner can do nothing to avert the inevitable sentence. As long as the tree remains evil it cannot produce good fruit. Is there, then, no hope for lost humanity? Wesley is certain there is hope – in the gospel,

---

[18]   J. Wesley, *Works [BE]*, Vol. 1, pp.225-227.

the good news, what he calls 'the whole revelation made to men by Jesus Christ.' Its substance is, 'Jesus Christ came into the world to save sinners.' Believe this, Wesley counsels, and the kingdom of God is yours.

> But it is, over and above this, a sure trust in the mercy of God through Jesus Christ. It is a confidence in a pardoning God. It is a divine evidence or conviction that 'God was in Christ, reconciling the world to himself, not imputing to them their former trespasses,' and in particular that the Son of God hath loved me and given himself for me; and that I, even I, am now reconciled to God by the blood of the cross.[19]

That this is a summary of the evangel John Wesley preached for fifty years is evident from all his publications. God loved the world and in grace and mercy he sent his Son to be the Saviour. By his life, and death, and resurrection, ascension and intercession, he made atonement for the sins of the world and that good news is now offered in the gospel. And that gospel is pre-eminently a gospel of grace; God comes to fallen mankind with the offer of forgiveness, sonship and the transforming energy of the Spirit. In a memorable and summary sentence, the 'grace or love of God.... is free in all and free for all.'[20] It is free in *all* because it does not depend on any power or merit in man; not on his endeavours, good works, righteousness or anything he is or does. These are but the streams, not the fountain; they are all 'the fruits of free grace and not the root.' Any good that is found in man or done by him, God is the author. This grace depends on God alone who freely gave his Son for the sins of the world. And it is free *for all* for no alleged secret decree can overturn God's purposes declared throughout all the Scriptures that he wills all men to be saved. A denial of this makes God unjust because it means that he condemns millions of souls to perdition for continuing in sin, 'which for want of that grace *he will not* give them, they cannot avoid.'[21]

---

[19] J .Wesley, *Works [BE]*, Vol. 1, p.230.
[20] J. Wesley, *Works [BE]*, Vol. 3, p.544.
[21] J. Wesley, *Works [BE]*, Vol. 3, p.555.

Although Wesley did not often use the *term* prevenient grace, the *idea* of preveniency is found everywhere in his soteriological writings. One of the most frequent charges made against his teaching on universal grace was that such a doctrine glorified the role of man's free will at the expense of the priority and sovereignty of God's grace. Wesley constantly replied that he taught, not natural free will but a *freed* will; men and women can respond to God's grace because they are given divine enablement. Natural free will in fallen man he denied, adding that he declared only 'a measure of free will supernaturally restored to every man, together with that supernatural light which enlightens every man that cometh into the world.'[22] He was attempting an *ordo salutis* from which a theological synergism emerged that combined the emphases that made salvation wholly of God's grace and mercy, and yet required a human response. Wesley had no doubt at all that he found both these elements in Scripture. His doctrine of grace, he replied to his critics, at every stage of its gracious operation, magnified the glory and honour of God. Nor did it impugn that honour by attributing the damnation of the lost to a divine decree. Men and women would be lost, not because God withheld his grace from them but because they spurned it in defiance and unbelief. As to how prevenient grace works in fallen humanity to bring sinners to salvation and eternal life, Wesley spelt out very carefully.

> His first step is to enlighten the understanding by that general knowledge of good and evil. To this he adds many secret reproofs, if they act contrary to this light; many inward convictions, which there is not a man on earth who hath not often felt.... He instils into their hearts good desires, though perhaps they know not from whence they come. Thus far he proceeds with all the children of men, yea, even with those who have not the knowledge of his written word. But in this, what a field of wisdom is displayed, suppose man to be in some degree a free agent. How is every part of it suited to this end, to save man, as man; to set life and death before him, and then persuade (not force) him to choose life.[23]

---

[22] J. Wesley, *The Works of John Wesley*, 14 Vols., London, 1872. Vol. 10, pp.229, 230. Hereafter cited as J. Wesley, *Works.*
[23] J. Wesley, 'Predestination Calmly Considerate,' Works, Vol. 10, p.232.

Given that John Wesley's *ordo salutis* had a very carefully laid foundation in universal sinfulness, both original and actual, it is not surprising that he reacted strongly to any attempt made to mitigate the disease or its consequences. For this reason he feared the harmful effects of the Enlightenment and humanistic optimism he charged on the teaching of the Socinian, Dr John Taylor. When Taylor published his attack on what was commonly accepted as the orthodox doctrine of original sin, Wesley waited in vain for someone to answer Taylor and then took up the cudgels himself. Taylor argued that the only consequence of Adam's sin in relation to mankind was physical death. He insisted that the Scriptures usually quoted in defence of the doctrine of original sin did not really bear that interpretation. There is no connection of any kind between Adam's sin and the sin of the world. We are all like Adam in that we have imitated his disobedience but he was in no sense our federal head, nor is there any Scripture that teaches, when rightly understood, any imputation of Adam's sin to the race or any suggestion of genetically-transmitted sinfulness. In particular Taylor found repugnant the idea that the guilt of Adam's sin should be charged against human beings. Men and women are responsible for their own sins and no one else's.

Wesley paid tribute to Taylor's well-deserved reputation for erudition and in particular his acknowledged expertise as a Hebrew exegete. But he paid no tribute to Taylor's Socinian anthropology. It was 'old Deism in a new dress,' sapping 'the very foundation of all revealed religion, whether Jewish or Christian.'[24] No one 'since Mahomet had given such a wound to Christianity,' and the poison has affected many of the clergy and the universities both in Britain and the Continent.[25] Wesley's vehement objection to Taylor's thesis was not only that it denied what he believed was Scripture's teaching on sin, but the consequences of that teaching threatened the whole Christian gospel. Taylor's scheme, with its Socinian doctrine of a reductionist Christology and its inevitable universalism, threatened all the doctrines of grace. In a personal letter to Taylor, he laid out the charge.

---

[24] J. Wesley, Preface, 'The Doctrine of Original Sin', *Works*, Vol. 9, pp.193, 194.
[25] J. Wesley, *Letters*, Vol. 4, p.48.

[This] controversy concerns a thing of the highest importance - nay, all the things that concern our eternal peace. It is Christianity or heathenism! for, take away the scriptural doctrine of Redemption or Justification, and that of the New Birth, the beginning of sanctification, or (which amounts to the same) explain them as you do, suitable to your doctrine of Original Sin, and what is Christianity better than Heathenism? Wherein, save in rectifying some of our notions, has the religion of St. Paul any pre-eminence over that of Socrates or Epictetus?[26]

Wesley followed up this reply to John Taylor two years later with a sermon entitled, *Original Sin*. It summarises the main points made in the longer work but it gave particular attention to how Taylor's scheme threatened the Christian doctrines of regeneration, justification and sanctification. Taylor's 'gospel' did not offer an adequate explanation for sin, either in its universal extent or its presence and power in the individual human heart. Natural man, that is, man without the influence of the Spirit on his mind and conscience, has no innate knowledge of God or of his own spiritual blindness. No man or woman understands the extent of their own spiritual perversion until their eyes are opened by the Spirit. If two infants were brought up from birth without having any religious instruction or any spiritual influence of any kind, they would have no more knowledge of God than 'the beasts of the field.... unless the grace of God interposed.'[27] The human heart is sinful and corrupt and this Adamic inheritance manifests itself in pride, idolatry, self-will and love of the world. The whole human race is fallen and this servitude to sin means that, apart from grace, men and women do not even recognise their enslavement to sin, much less are they able to break free from it. It is this doctrine of mankind's universal revolt from God, claims Wesley that distinguishes Christianity from every form of heathenism, past and present.

Dr Taylor's denial of original sin leads inevitably to a denial of the Scripture teaching on the need of the new birth and regeneration. Wesley was no doubt remembering a visit he had paid a year earlier to

---

[26] J. Wesley, *Letters*, Vol. 4, p.67.
[27] J .Wesley, *Works [BE]*, Vol. 2, pp.177, 178.

Dr Taylor's meetinghouse in Norwich. He observed then that it was probably the 'most elegant' of its kind in all Europe, its architecture and furnishings were of the finest quality and even 'the very latches of the pew doors are polished brass.' Wesley then added dryly: 'How can it be thought that the old, coarse Gospel should find admission here?'[28] Now in his sermon he alleged that Taylor's Socinianism was inimical to all the doctrines of grace. Where the gospel of Christ is not preached men and women continue in their sleep of spiritual death. The true Christian faith, proclaiming the Scripture doctrines of sin, grace, faith, regeneration by the Spirit and the gift of eternal life, is alone a *therapeia psuches* – a healing of the soul. All other religions fail both in diagnosis of the human malady and in offering an effective remedy. Wesley warned of that 'poor farce and mere mockery of God' that is offered when the doctrines of grace are denied. But he went further and warned against those 'teachers of lies' who come with 'all smoothness of language, all decency, yea, beauty and elegance of expression.'[29] This thrust at Dr Taylor and all his Socinian sympathisers was only slightly veiled. Then in a moving plea to his readers and hearers to return to what he called 'the plain old faith,' John Wesley concluded his sermon with a passionate plea that united his doctrines of original sin and prevenient grace.

> Keep to the plain, old 'faith, once delivered to the saints,' and delivered by the Spirit of God to your hearts. Know your disease! Know your cure! Ye were born in sin: Therefore, 'Ye must be born again, born of God.' By nature ye are wholly corrupted: By grace ye shall be wholly renewed. 'In Adam ye all died:' In the second Adam, 'in Christ, ye all are made alive.' You 'that were dead in sins hath he quickened:' He hath already given you a principle of life, even 'faith in him who loved *you* and gave himself for *you*.' Now 'go on' 'from faith to faith,' until your whole sickness be healed, and all that 'mind be in you which was also in Christ Jesus.'[30]

---

[28] J. Wesley, *The Journal of The Rev. John Wesley*, Vol. 4, p.244. Hereafter cited as J. Wesley, *Journal*.
[29] J. Wesley, *Works [BE]*, Vol. 2, p.185.
[30] J Wesley, *Works [BE]*, Vol. 2, p.185.

John Wesley's controversy with John Taylor in the late 1750s highlighted the relationship between the doctrine of original sin and the other doctrines of grace. It has, however, been noted already that Wesley's concern to understand biblical anthropology went back to his years in Oxford. He continued to read and study on these matters into the early years of the revival and the first Conference of his preachers, convened in 1744, gave attention to it. The theological discussions between the Wesley brothers and the gathered preachers were carried on in question and answer form. One of the questions asked how the sin of Adam is imputed to the whole race. The agreed answer was:

> In Adam all die; that is, (1). Our bodies then became mortal. (2). Our souls died; that is, were disunited from God. And hence, (3). We are all born with a sinful, devilish nature. By reason whereof, (4). We are children of wrath, liable to death eternal. (Rom. 5:18; Ephes. 2:3.)[31]

The wide popularity of Taylor's doctrines convinced Wesley that a strong emphasis on the doctrine of original sin was the only way to secure the biblical doctrines of justification and sanctification alone by faith in Jesus Christ. As essentially a practical theologian he knew that Taylor's smooth-tongued Socinian optimism about mankind must be rebutted on two fronts. There was need, as he had attempted, to answer Taylor's specious arguments page by page, but there was even more need to press the unrelenting work of proclaiming the gospel throughout the kingdom. At the same time, the on-going dispute with high Calvinism posed another pressing question for Wesley. How was it possible to hold, as he did, a near-Augustinian doctrine of original sin without holding to unconditional election? If fallen man was as wholly sinful and spiritually helpless as Wesley's doctrine of original sin certainly entailed, then how could sinners make any response to God's grace? High Calvinism solved that dilemma with its doctrine of limited atonement, arguing that Christ died only for the elect; saving grace is offered only to the elect, and, having been eternally elected, they are enabled to respond to that grace. Wesley was as convinced as any Calvinist about the nature and extent of original sin. Fallen man is both sinful and helpless, but no man is excluded from the love of

---

[31] J. Wesley, *Works*, Vol. 8, p.277.

God by an eternal decree. How, then, can the helpless sinner respond to the grace of God? If he does respond, does this not suggest some Pelagian notion of innate ability? Wesley's opponents repeatedly charged him with being Pelagian, asserting that the only alternative to unconditional election was the Pelagian heresy of salvation by man's free will rather than by God's free grace.

Wesley's answer to this charge was to re-assert his doctrine of prevenient grace. He had no doubt that Scripture taught, at one and the same time, both the sinfulness of man and his responsibility to respond to divine grace. On that response depended his salvation; no man would be lost by a divine unalterable decree that determined his damnation; rather he would be lost because he refused the grace offered to him. Convinced that by the doctrine of original sin Christianity stands or falls, Wesley steered a course that sought to avoid both the determinist implications of high Calvinism and the rationalist tendencies of Pelagianism. Throughout a long ministry he was sure that Scripture presented a doctrine of divine intervention and grace that was properly labelled 'preventing' or 'prevenient.'

When the 1744 Conference debated the question of the imputation of Adam's sin, it led to the question of the meaning of Rom. 5:19. In Wesley's New Testament text it read, 'For as by the disobedience of one man, many were constituted sinners, so by the obedience of one, many shall be constituted righteous.'[32] While the agreed conclusion did not use the term prevenient grace, it was certainly the implication drawn from this biblical text.

> That text we conceive means, By the merits of Christ, all men are cleared from the guilt of Adam's actual sin. We conceive farther, that through the obedience and death of Christ, (1). The bodies of all men become immortal after the resurrection. (2). Their souls receive a capacity of spiritual life, and, (3). An actual spark or seed thereof. (4). All believers become children of grace, reconciled to God; and, (5). Made partakers of the divine nature.[33]

---

[32] J. Wesley, *Explanatory Notes upon The New Testament*, 1754, Romans 5:19.
[33] J. Wesley, *Works*, Vol. 8, pp.277, 278.

The first sentence in this summary is the key to how Wesley and his preachers understood Paul's teaching here on the Adam/Christ relationship. 'By the merits of Christ all men are cleared from the guilt of Adam's actual sin.' The words 'all men' are meant to denote the entire human race to the end of time. Christ's death has effected for them the removal of the guilt inherited from Adam. Wesley never wavered in his assertion that the race suffers the consequences of Adam's sin but those consequences do not include the guilt incurred by Adam himself. In a later letter he enlarged on this interpretation. When Rom. 5:18 says that by one offence, judgement came upon all, it means that 'condemnation affects every infant as well as every adult person. But it is equally true that "by the righteousness of one, the free gift came upon all men," all born into the world, infant or adult, unto justification. Therefore no infant ever was, or ever will be "sent to hell for the guilt of Adam's sin," seeing it is cancelled by the righteousness of Christ as soon as they are sent into the world.'[34]

It can be inferred from this explanation that Wesley is certain that Christ's righteousness effects a cancellation of Adam's guilt for all his posterity. No man or woman will be finally condemned on account of Adam's sin; their condemnation will be the consequence of their own continued impenitence. Clearly Wesley interpreted both Adam and Christ as being representatives of the whole race. Adam, as a representative, brought universal condemnation in his 'Fall,' and Christ, representing all mankind, brought justification, in the sense of a mitigation of the consequences of Adam's sin. Although Wesley does not say that he uses the words 'justified' and 'justification' at two levels of meaning, yet he clearly does. At one level, the whole race is justified because Christ has cancelled the guilt of Adam's they would otherwise have inherited. At a higher level, only those who personally and deliberately repent and believe in Christ are justified unto eternal life. This is the level of justification he means when he preaches and teaches justification by faith. The former level refers to a gift conferred on the whole race, without their request or consent, as the outcome of Christ's atoning death. Wesley never ceased to emphasise that Christ's

---

[34] J. Wesley, *Letters*, Vol. 6, pp.239, 240.

death was universal in its efficacy, so it can be logically inferred that he meant that all men and women are potentially saved. But Wesley's concept of universal prevenient grace did not slide imperceptibly into universalism. His doctrine did mean, however, that all men are constituted salvable by the efficacy of that grace that flows from the work of Christ.

In an important soteriological sermon published in 1785, John Wesley attempted to show the scriptural relationship between the divine initiative, viz, prevenient grace, and the sinner's responsibility and enabled ability to respond to grace. The sermon was based on Phil. 2:12, 13 'Work out your own salvation…. for it is God that worketh in you…' Fifty years earlier he had commended William Tilly's exposition of these verses and while his own interpretation now followed similar lines to Tilly's, it was much more a worked-out *ordo salutis* than the former treatment.

> Salvation begins with what is usually termed (and very properly) 'preventing grace;' including the first wish to please God, the first dawn of light concerning his will, and the first, slight, transient conviction of having sinned against him. All these imply some tendency toward life, some degree of salvation, the beginning of a deliverance from a blind, unfeeling heart, quite insensible of God and the things of God. Salvation is carried on by 'convincing grace,' usually in Scripture termed 'repentance,' which brings a larger measure of self knowledge, and a further deliverance from the heart of stone. Afterwards we experience the proper Christian salvation, whereby 'through grace' we 'are saved by faith,' consisting of those two grand branches, justification and sanctification.[35]

John Wesley's explication of how prevenient grace is the gift of God to the whole race through Christ involves his understanding of the nature and purpose of God's law. While he deals with this in many of his writings, his 1750 sermon, *The Original, Nature, Property, and Use of the Law*, was his clearest summary of it. God gave this law, a full reflection of his own perfection, to angels and to Adam and Eve. For Adam it was not written in stone tablets but rather 'engraved on

---

[35] J. Wesley, *Works [BE]*, Vol. 3, pp.203, 204.

his heart by the finger of God.' It was 'an incorruptible picture of the High and Holy One that inhabiteth eternity.... It is the face of God unveiled.... It is the heart of God disclosed to man.'[36] In *The Righteousness of Faith*, preached by Wesley at least seven times between 1740 and 1789, that man 'should fulfil all righteousness .... That he should continue holy as He which had created him was holy' and he should be 'perfect as his Father in heaven is perfect.' It also required that he should love 'the Lord his God with all his soul, mind and strength; that he should love every soul which God had made, even as God had loved him.'[37]

When Adam sinned, he broke this glorious law and though it resulted in darkness in his soul and alienation from God, he was not left in that condition. God, reconciled to man, through the Son of his love, 're-inscribed the law on the heart of His dark, sinful creature.'[38] This is Wesley's language for prevenient grace for the reconciliation between God and man is through the Son of his love. When the whole world lay in spiritual darkness, God gave this law to Moses and through him to the elect nation of Israel. Then, when the fullness of time had come, God sent his Son, who came, not to destroy the law but to fulfil it perfectly. This law convinces the world of sin. It 'slays the sinner,' convinces him that he is dead while he lives and then, as a schoolmaster, brings him to Christ.

Given John Wesley's picture of the spiritual blindness and helplessness of the unregenerate man, how does this law work on his heart? By what means does the sinner become conscious that he is a sinner, that is, a transgressor of God's holy law? How does prevenient grace begin to illuminate his heart and mind to bring about conviction of sin? Wesley's answer is – by conscience. He defined it as 'a faculty or power, implanted by God in every soul that comes into the world, of perceiving what is right or wrong in his own heart or life, in his

---

[36] J. Wesley, *Works [BE]*, Vol. 2, p.9.
[37] J .Wesley, *Works [BE]*, Vol. 1, pp.204, 205.
[38] J. Wesley, *Works [BE]*, Vol. 2, p.7.

tempers, thoughts, words and actions.'[39] For all those without the knowledge of the revelation of God, the faculty works by what Paul referred to as the law written in the heart.

> 'These, (saith he) not having the (outward) law, are a law unto themselves: who show the work of the law,' that which the outward law prescribes, 'written in their heart,' by the finger of God: 'their conscience also bearing' whether they walk by this rule or not; 'and their thoughts the meanwhile accusing, or even excusing,' acquitting, defending them. But the Christian rule of right and wrong is the Word, the writings of the Old and New Testament: all which the prophets and holy men of God wrote as they were moved by the Holy Ghost.[40]

Wesley is adamant that this capacity for discernment between right and wrong is not some remaining vestige of the *imago Dei* in fallen man, nor is it something innate in human nature. Rather it is the working of prevenient grace. It is commonly referred to as 'natural conscience,' and Wesley accepts the adjective 'natural,' as long as it means only that it is found universally. 'Properly speaking it is not *natural*; but a supernatural gift of God, above all his natural endowments. No, it is not nature but the Son of God that is 'the true light, which enlighteneth every man which cometh into the world.'[41] The discernment between right and wrong which prevenient grace bestows is not a foundation on which to build a *theologia naturalis*. Prevenient grace is not saving grace nor does it give any knowledge of the distinctly Christian doctrines of Christology and pneumatology.[42]

This understanding of prevenient grace as God's gracious gift of moral discernment given to all mankind enabled Wesley to hold in tension his insistence on both the divine initiative in salvation and the responsibility of sinners to respond to grace. He saw very clearly that an over-emphasis on human depravity nullified man's responsibility, while an over-emphasis on human ability supported Pelagian optimism. He was convinced that the doctrine of prevenient grace

---

[39] J. Wesley, *Works [BE]*, Vol. 1, p.302.
[40] J. Wesley, *Works [BE]*, Vol. 1, pp.302, 303.
[41] J. Wesley, *Works [BE]*, Vol. 3, p.482.
[42] J. Wesley, *Works [BE]*, Vol. 3, p.200.

meant that a scriptural balance could be maintained between original sin on one hand and human responsibility on the other. His clearest enunciation of this theological balance came in his 1785 sermon, *On Working Out Our Own Salvation.*

> Allowing that all the souls of men are dead in sin by nature, this excuses none, seeing there is no man that is in a state of mere nature; there is no man, unless he has quenched the Spirit, that is wholly void of the grace of God. No man living is entirely destitute of what is vulgarly called 'natural conscience.' But this is not natural; it is more properly termed 'preventing grace.' Every man has a greater or less measure of this, which waiteth not for the call of man. Everyone has sooner or later good desires, although the generality of men stifle them before they can strike deep root or produce any considerable fruit. Everyone has some measure of that light, some faith glimmering ray, which sooner or later, more or less, enlightens every man that cometh into the world.... No man sins because he has not grace, but because he does not use the grace which he hath.[43]

John Wesley claimed that his doctrine of salvation was a doctrine of grace from beginning to end. God, in his love and mercy, reached out to all men and had, from the Fall in Eden, made provision for their salvation. Through the atonement for sin made by the Son of his love, he had mitigated the consequences of the Fall and had enabled sinners to respond to his further overtures of grace. His *ordo salutis* embraced what might be called the stages of grace.

> Salvation begins with what is usually termed (and very properly) 'preventing grace,' including the first wish to please God, the first dawn of light concerning his will, and the first slight, transient conviction of having sinned against him. All these imply some tendency toward life, some degree of salvation, the beginning of a deliverance from a blind, unfeeling heart, quite insensible to God and the things of God. Salvation is carried on by 'convincing grace,' usually in Scripture termed 'repentance.'.... Afterwards we experience the proper Christian salvation, whereby, 'through grace,' we 'are saved by faith,' consisting of those two grand branches, justification and sanctification.[44]

---

[43] J. Wesley, *Works [BE]*, Vol. 3, p.207.
[44] J. Wesley, *Works [BE]*, Vol. 3, pp.203, 204.

Although John Wesley did not write an extensive treatise on the person and work of the Holy Spirit, yet all his writings are replete with references to the ministry of the Spirit. The Spirit is active at every stage in man's redemption, from the first stirrings of an awakened conscience in the sinner to the Christian's final entry into glory. The role and action of the Spirit in Wesley's explication of the doctrine of prevenient grace is particularly significant, giving that doctrine both a Christological and a pneumatological foundation. Evaluating the distinctives of Wesleyan teaching, James Orr concluded that while Wesleyanism is usually classed with Arminianism, yet it essentially differs from it 'in the central place it gives to the work of the Spirit in regeneration.'[45] While this comparison is indisputable in terms of the Arminianism of many of Arminius' followers, John Wesley gave great prominence to the work of the Spirit in the various stages of spiritual awakening that precede regeneration.

As early as his 1733 Oxford sermon, 'The Circumcision of the Heart,' Wesley stressed the role of the Spirit in man's redemption. Such is the condition of fallen man that apart from the gracious intervention and assistance of divine grace he is hopelessly lost in sin.

> Without the Spirit of God, we can do nothing but add sin to sin; it is He alone who worketh in us by His almighty power, either to will or do that which is good; it being impossible for us even to think a good thought, without the supernatural assistance of His Spirit, as to create ourselves, or to renew our whole souls in righteousness and true holiness.... This is that lowliness of mind which they have learned of Christ who follow his example and tread in his steps. And this knowledge of their disease, whereby that are more and more cleansed from one part of it, pride and vanity, disposes them to embrace with a willing mind the second thing implied in 'circumcision of heart' - that faith which alone is able to make them whole, which is the one medicine given under heaven to heal their sickness.[46]

---

45 J. Orr, *The Progress of Dogma*, 1897, p.300.
46 J. Wesley, *Works [BE]*, Vol. 1, pp.403, 404.

Later in the sermon Wesley reiterated how the Spirit must initiate the work of salvation in the heart. Quoting Paul's words that without the Spirit no man is truly a Christian, he stressed that the Spirit alone can quicken those who are spiritually dead. He added that only the Spirit can breathe into them what he calls 'the breath of Christian life, and so prevent, accompany, and follow them with his graces to bring their good desires to good effect.'[47] By 'prevent' Wesley meant the prevenient activity of the Holy Spirit in bringing about the very first spiritual awakening and awareness in the sinner. Arthur Skevington Wood drew a parallel between John Wesley's teaching on the Spirit's prevenient work and the teaching of Luther and Calvin at this point.

> In his sermons Wesley spoke of the Spirit's gracious activity at every stage of man's experience of God. If in his insistence on justification Wesley trod in the steps of Martin Luther, in this repeated emphasis on the Holy Spirit as the prior agent of effectual calling he was reminiscent of John Calvin. But whereas Calvin and his disciples regarded regeneration as the initial work of the Spirit as He implants new life in the soul, Wesley resorted to the doctrine of prevenient grace, in which the Spirit exerts what might be described as pre-natal influences.[48]

When John Wesley described his doctrines of grace as coming 'within a hair's breadth' of Calvinism, he was confirming his emphasis on man's fallen state, his separation from God and his total inability, apart from grace, to make any move towards salvation. On the other hand he rejected the suggestion that the unregenerate man is 'as dead as stone,' because, he argued, there is no man living 'without some preventing grace, and every degree of grace is a degree of life.'[49] Prevenient grace is not saving grace but it is the first step on the way to life eternal. It is the gift of God's love, mediated by the work of Christ and applied by the Spirit. It can be resisted and all the overtures of grace to the soul spurned and betrayed, but equally, where it is embraced and followed, it leads the soul to light and truth and eventually to salvation. Wesley was convinced that his understanding of prevenient grace enabled him

---

[47] J. Wesley, *Works [BE]*, Vol 1, p.411.
[48] A. S. Wood, *The Burning Heart: John Wesley, Evangelist*, 1967, p.241.
[49] J. Wesley, *Letters,* Vol. 6, p.239.

to hold an orthodox doctrine of original sin which nevertheless did not logically lead to absolute predestination. And neither did it lead to Pelagianism, for every wish, desire and aspiration in the human heart for anything that is good is because of that grace that always goes before human endeavour. It is undeniable that Wesley's doctrine has the most profound implications for a theology of mission. It not only claims a universal atonement for human sin in the person and work of Christ, but it also claims that God's Spirit is at work in the soul of every human being, unless that soul has quenched the prevenient ministry of awakening and illuminating. Wesley did not develop his doctrine in any significant way in terms of what it says about other world religions, though he asserted over and over again that salvation is in Christ alone. In terms of his own half-century of mission in Britain, it meant, as Skevington Wood observed, that 'God's salvation may be extended to all because his grace is already incipiently at work in all.'[50] Two final quotations from John Wesley's writings illustrate how he believed that he had secured a scriptural balance as he structured his *ordo salutis*. Early in the work of the revival, in his 1745 apologia, *A Farther Appeal to Men of Reason and Religion*, he spoke of how the Spirit of God prompts and enables the sinner's search for light and truth at every instant.

> The author of faith and salvation is God alone. It is he that works in us both to will and to do. He is the sole giver of every good gift, and the sole Author of every good work. There is no more of power than of merit in man; but as all merit is in the Son of God, in what he has done and suffered for us, so all power is in the Spirit of God. And therefore every man, in order to believe unto salvation, must receive the Holy Ghost.... Sometimes He acts on the wills and affections of men; withdrawing them from evil, inclining them to good.... It is certain [that] all true faith, and the whole work of salvation, every good thought, word, and work, is altogether by the operation of the Spirit of God.[51]

---

[50] A. S. Wood, 'The Contribution of John Wesley to the Theology of Grace,' *Grace Unlimited*, Edited by C. Pinnock, 1975, p.216.
[51] J. Wesley, *Works [BE]*, Vol. 11, pp.107, 108.

This argument was made in answer to those who challenged Wesley's doctrine of salvation by faith and his claims that the Spirit bears witness in the believer's heart that he is born of God. In particular he was replying to the charge that this interpretation of salvation by faith was a denial of the Church of England's doctrine of baptism. Wesley was certain that in giving priority to the work of the Spirit in man's salvation he was in harmony with both Scripture and the teaching of the Articles and Homilies. Nearly thirty years later, in the midst of an internecine strife between Wesleyan and Calvinist Methodists, he was being branded by some as 'an enemy of grace.' His insistence that the justifying and sanctifying work of the Spirit in Christians must result in good works and holiness of life, was being castigated as a Romanist doctrine of salvation by works. Wesley's reply was that for more than three decades he had proclaimed the doctrines of salvation by faith through grace with consistency and conviction.

> I did always for between these thirty and forty years clearly assert the total fall of man and his utter inability to do any good of himself; the absolute necessity of the grace and Spirit of God to raise even a good thought or desire in our hearts; the Lord's rewarding no work and accepting of none but so far as they proceed from His preventing, convincing, and converting grace through the Beloved; the blood and righteousness of Christ being the sole meritorious cause of our salvation. Who is there in England that has asserted these things more strongly and steadily than I have done?[52]

The hymns of Charles Wesley put the doctrines and experiences of the Methodist Revival on the lips of thousands of people. Very early in the revival Charles wrote a hymn entitled, *Free Grace*. It was destined to become one of the most popular of his immense output of hymns and two and a half centuries later it is still being sung by the people of God around the world. One verse expresses in poetic vein the doctrine of prevenient grace that both brothers preached so fervently.

> Long my imprisoned spirit lay
> Fast bound in sin and nature's night.
> Thine eye diffused a quickening ray

---

[52] J. Wesley, *Letters*, Vol. 5, p.231.

I woke, the dungeon flamed with light
My chains fell off, my heart was free
I rose, went forth, and followed Thee.[53]

[53] John and Charles Wesley, *The Poetical Works of John and Charles Wesley*, 1868, Vol. 1, p.105.

SCRIPTURAL HOLINESS –
THE METHODIST DISTINCTIVE

Among the previously delivered Maynard James Memorial Lectures have been those dealing with biblical and theological interests that were central to the ministry of Maynard James. These have included such subjects as biblical prophecy, evangelism, and the work and ministry of the Holy Spirit. No less significant was the place Maynard James gave to the doctrine of Christian holiness. Throughout his long ministry as preacher, evangelist and founder/editor of *The Flame* magazine, he advocated the Wesleyan understanding of holiness with passion and conviction. It was this conviction which was expressed in *The Flame's* subtitle, 'A Bi-Monthly Magazine for the Spread of Full Salvation,' which first appeared in 1935. The first 'Editorial' set out, as one of the aims:

> To proclaim, through the medium of the printed page, the glorious truth of holiness; this is our passion in sending forth The Flame.... Sin in its two fold aspect, indwelling and actual, has been dealt with on Calvary.... Every child of God, conscious of inward depravity, can be entirely sanctified by faith, through the operation of the baptism with the Holy Spirit. This, we are convinced, is the plain teaching of Scripture. We take our stand with Wesley, Fox, Booth, and host of other witnesses on the lines of full salvation.[54]

James B. Maclagan, writing in *The Flame* in the first issue, on 'Holiness: Our Business', points to the Methodists as having the same doctrine.

> What is true of Methodism with respect to the precious doctrine of entire sanctification, or the experience of holiness in heart and life, is also true of the Holiness Movements throughout this land. This is the purpose for which we exist; and aside from this it matters very little about us. We are not called to advance new theories, or to speculation in any field of thought. We are called of God to spread scriptural holiness over our beloved land. When we cease to do this - if we do cease - and turn aside to other things our mission is ended. It is the earnest prayer of the writer that the Holy Spirit may bear this solemn

---

[54] *The Flame*, Vol. 1, No. 1, April-May, 1935, p.2.

thrust into the hearts of all who are in any way connected with the spreading of full salvation, and that subsequent editions of *The Flame* will witness to the glorious experience of entire sanctification is such a clear and definite way that it will be used to the bringing of many into the blessing.[55]

Two writers of the same movements point to this doctrine as the very truth that God raised them up. What was true in 18th century Methodism has again been brought to the fore and it is transparent that the 1930 evangelists were well known for searching out Wesley's doctrine. When James published his first book in 1945, *Evangelise*, dealing with 'Past and Present Methods of Soul-winning,' he devoted one chapter to what he called 'The Holiness Emphasis.' Drawing attention to passages from John Wesley's writings where he had written of the link between the sanctification of believers and the general spread of the gospel, Maynard James concluded: 'Wesley taught that the preaching of holiness was a distinct factor in evangelism; that the entire sanctification of Christians resulted in more effective soul-winning.'[56] Two years later he published his second book, *Facing The Issue*, and the final chapter was entitled 'The Secret of Sanctification.' Rather than a discussion on the nature of Christian holiness, this was an evangelistic attempt to encourage and guide every Christian into the highway of holiness.

When William Sangster's book, *The Path to Perfection*, appeared in 1943, Maynard James was sure it misrepresented Wesley's teaching on entire sanctification, and in a very trenchant review in *The Flame* he said so. Not only had Sangster failed to take into account the full Scriptural teaching on the nature of original sin but he had also failed to do justice to John Wesley's teaching on the possibility of being saved from sin in this life.

> We are compelled to regard Dr Sangster's new book as 'a path to confusion and not as 'the *Path to Perfection*.'' No shame need be ours if we, like the great John Wesley, continue to proclaim to all seekers

---

[55] James B. Maclagen, 'Holiness: Our Business,' *The Flame*, Vol. 1. No. 1, April-May, 1035, p.2.
[56] Maynard James, *Evangelise*, 1945, p.40.

after perfect purity that 'If you are simple of heart, if you are willing to receive the heavenly gift as a little child, without reasoning, why may you not receive it now?'[57]

His longest book was his 1965 publication, *I Believe in the Holy Ghost*, and it contained chapters entitled 'The Sanctifying Spirit' and 'The Pentecost of Romans,' that gave a clear Wesleyan exposition of these themes. Forty-nine years after he launched *The Flame*, Maynard James wrote his final editorial in the January-February, 1984 issue. Making a strong plea that the Holiness Churches would, in his words, keep 'the teaching and spirit of Scripture and of John Wesley himself,' he argued: 'As Holiness people and professed descendants of John Wesley, we should be in a position to take with joy and divine conviction the glorious Bible truth of entire sanctification to other sections of the Christian Church.'[58] These extracts amply demonstrate that Maynard James was fully committed to John Wesley's teaching on Christian holiness, and so an analysis of that teaching is surely an apt subject for the Maynard James Memorial Lecture. This Lecture will concentrate on looking chronologically at Wesley's teaching on Christian holiness across more than fifty years and will examine how consistent was that teaching in a lifetime of preaching and writing.

In a letter written to Robert Carr Brackenbury on September 15, 1789, John Wesley penned the often-quoted words: 'I am glad Brother Dieuside has more light with regard to full sanctification. This doctrine is the grand depositum which God has lodged with the people called Methodists; and for the sake of propagating this chiefly He appeared to have raised us up.'[59] Four months before he died he wrote to Adam Clarke. 'If we can prove that any of our local Preachers or Leaders, either directly or indirectly, speak against it, let him be a Local Preacher or Leader no longer. I doubt whether he shall continue in the

---

[57] Maynard James, *The Flame*, Vol. 9, No. 3, April-May, 1935, p.27. I am indebted to the Revd. Andrew Cheatle, Manchester, for drawing my attention to this review.

[58] Maynard James, *The Flame*, Vol. 50, No. 1, p.18.

[59] J. Wesley, *Letters*, Vol. 8, p.238.

Society.' Because he that can speak thus in our congregations cannot be an honest man.[60]

These two quotations from John Wesley, selected from many similar pronouncements, show how important he believed the doctrine of Christian holiness to be. The significance of these entries is that it was repeated at every Conference for the next twenty-six years; John Wesley intended to remind all his preachers that their great mission was the dissemination of the doctrine and practice of scriptural holiness throughout Britain. Through a long ministry Wesley preached scriptural holiness, explained it, urged his preachers to declare it, and defended it from misunderstanding within and overt attack from without, the Methodist Societies. He always dated his own spiritual pilgrimage from 1725, the year of his ordination, when he began to read Jeremy Taylor's, *Rule and Exercise of Holy Living and Dying.* His 1766 publication, *A Plain Account of Christian Perfection,* opens with the explanation:

> What I purpose in the following papers is to give a plain and distinct account of the steps by which I was led, during a course of many years, to embrace the doctrine of Christian perfection. This I owe to the serious part of mankind, those who desire to know all the truth as it is in Jesus. And these only are concerned in questions of this kind. To these I would nakedly declare the thing as it is, endeavouring all along to show, from one period to another, both what I thought, and why I thought so.[61]

The first step Wesley enumerated was his 1725 reading of Jeremy Taylor. This work convinced him of the need of 'purity of intention.' 'Instantly I resolved to dedicate all my life to God; all my thoughts and words and action, being thoroughly convinced, there was no medium; but that every part of my life must either be a sacrifice to God, or myself, that is, in effect, to the devil.'[62] Taylor's writings had a profound and long-lasting influence on Wesley's thinking and practice. As well as being instrumental in prompting Wesley to begin

---

[60] J. Wesley, *Letters*, Vol. 8, p.249.
[61] J. Wesley, *Works*, Vol. 11, p.366.
[62] J. Wesley, *Works*, Vol. 11, p.366.

keeping a private *Diary* from 1725 and a more famous *Journal* from 1735, Taylor set John Wesley on the search for personal holiness. That quest and exploration never ceased to be a part of Wesley's spiritual pilgrimage, and after 1738 in particular it issued in the preaching of that doctrine of scriptural holiness to which the bishop's writings had introduced him. In a 1765 letter to John Newton, answering a question about the origins of his understanding of Christian perfection, Wesley wrote:

> But how came this opinion into my mind? I will tell you with all simplicity. In 1725 I met with Bishop Taylor's *Rules of Holy Living and Dying*. I was struck particularly with the chapter upon Intention, and felt a fixed intention to *give myself up to God*. In this I was much confirmed soon after by the *Christian Pattern*, and longed to give God all my heart. This is just what I mean by perfection now: I sought after it from that hour. In 1727 I read Mr. Law's *Christian Perfection* and *Serious Call*, and more explicitly resolved to be all devoted to God in body, soul and spirit. In 1730 I began to be homo *unius libri*, to study no book but the Bible. I then saw in a stronger light than ever before that only one thing is needful, even faith that worketh by the love of God and man, all inward and outward holiness; and I groaned to love God with all my heart and to serve Him with all my strength.[63]

What is often overlooked is what Wesley wrote immediately after acknowledging his indebtedness to Taylor and Law.

> In the year 1729, I began not only to read, but to study, the Bible, as the one, the only standard of truth, and the only model of pure religion. Hence I saw, in a clearer and clearer light, the indispensable necessity of having 'the mind which was in Christ,' and of 'walking as Christ also walked;' even of having, not some part only, but all the mind which was in him; and of walking as he walked, not only in many or is some respects, but in all things. And this was the light, wherein at this time I generally considered religion, as a uniform following of Christ, an entire inward and outward conformity to our Master.[64]

It would not be too much to say that from 1725 John Wesley pursued Christian holiness for the rest of his life; and he probably would have

---

[63] J. Wesley, *Letters*, Vol. 4, pp.298, 299.
[64] J. Wesley, *Works*, Vol. 11, p.367.

been quite happy to hear that doctrine characterised as 'the Wesleyan distinctive.'[65]

When Wesley published his *Plain Account* in 1766 it was not an original publication. On purpose it was a bringing together of what he had been writing on Christian holiness since 1741. Many who were antagonistic to this teaching were charging Wesley with inconsistency, contradictions and confusion, and Wesley's reply was to issue his most definitive essay on the subject up until that time. He set out to show that his teaching had not changed in twenty-five years, and as well as citing from his earlier writings he also added some new material in the form of textual exposition. In all, his *Plain Account* was re-issued four times in his lifetime and it remains his fullest treatment on Christian holiness. To him this subject was no mere theological abstraction; it was no provincialism of Methodism; rather it was the highway of holiness where God required all His people to walk. Scriptural holiness is purity of intention, giving God all our heart, inward and outward cleansing, having the mind that was in Christ, being renewed in the image of God and loving God and our neighbour.

Near the end of his *Plain Account*, Wesley dwells on what he has found and encourages all his people to seek and find this glorious experience.

It is the doctrine of St. Paul, the doctrine of St. James, of St. Peter, and St. John; and no otherwise Mr. Wesley's, than as it is the doctrine of every one who preaches the pure and the whole gospel. I tell you, as plain as I can speak, where and when I found this. I found it in the oracles of God, in the Old and New Testaments; when I read them with no other view or desire but to save my own soul. But whosoever this doctrine is, I pray you, what harm is there in it?.... In one view, it is purity of intention, dedicating all the life to God. It is giving God all our heart; it is one desire and deign ruling our tempers. It is the

---

[65] Writing to a member of one of the Methodist Societies in 1774, Wesley spoke of the great harm done to the work of God in England by the spread of Antinomianism. Then he added: 'But God has already lifted up His standard, and He will maintain His own cause. In the present dispensation He is undoubtedly aiming at that point, to spread holiness over the land. It is our wisdom to have this always in view, inward and outward holiness.' *Letters*, Vol. 6, p.113.

devoting, not a part, but all our souls, body and substance to God. In another view, it is all the mind which was in Christ, enabling us to walk as Christ walked. It is the circumcision of the heart, from all filthiness, all inward as well as outward pollution. It is the renewal of the heart in the whole image of God, the full likeness of Him that created it. In yet another, it is the loving God with all our heart, and our neighbour as ourselves.[66]

Three other important sources must also be mentioned. First, Wesley's 1755 *Explanatory Notes Upon the New Testament;* second, the various hymn books published by both brothers, especially the 'Prefaces,' and, third, John Wesley's statements, exhortations, explanations and replies to questions in his *Letters.*

As noted earlier, one of Wesley's early mentors was the Non-Juror, William Law, and it is significant that the post-1738 John Wesley became less and less enamoured of some of Law's teaching. This was mainly because Wesley blamed Law with confusing justification and sanctification. Years later, in his 1787 sermon, *On God's Vineyard,* Wesley wrote:

> It is true a very late, eminent author in his strange treatise on regeneration, proceeds entirely on the supposition that it is the whole, gradual progress of sanctification. No; it is only the threshold of sanctification, the first entrance upon it. And as in the natural birth a man is born at once, and then grows larger and stronger by degrees, so in the spiritual birth a man is born at once, and then gradually increases in spiritual stature and strength. The new birth, therefore, is the first point of sanctification, which may increase more and more unto the perfect day.[67]

Perhaps no area of John Wesley's theological thought needs to be more clearly enunciated than this; that the new birth is holiness begun. In the sermon, *On God's Vineyard,* he draws a distinction between Methodists and Church of England.

---

[66]   J. Wesley, *Works*, Vol. 11, pp.444. 190.
[67]   J. Wesley, *Works [BE]*, Vol. 3, 507.

It has pleased God to give the Methodists a full and clear knowledge of each, and the wide difference between them. They know indeed that at the time a man is justified sanctification properly begins. For when he is justified he is 'born again,' 'born of the Spirit,' it is doubtless the gate of it.... It is true that a late eminent author, in his strange treatise on regeneration, proceeds entirely on the supposition that it is the whole, gradual progress of sanctification.[68] No, it is only the threshold of sanctification – the first entrance upon it. As in the natural birth a man is born at once, and then larger and stronger by degrees, so in the spiritual birth a man is born at once, and then gradually increases in spiritual stature and strength. The new birth, therefore, is the first point of sanctification, which may increase more and more unto the perfect day.... Therefore they maintain with equal zeal and diligence the doctrine of free, full, present justification on the one hand, and of entire sanctification both of heart and life on the other.[69]

John Wesley's understanding of justification by faith is important, both in its own right and because his doctrine of sanctification is so dependent upon it. There is no clearer statement on it anywhere in his writings than his 1746 sermon, *Justification By Faith*.

The plain scriptural notion of justification is pardon, the forgiveness of sins. It is that act of God the Father, whereby, for the sake of the propitiation made by the blood of his Son, he 'showeth forth his righteousness (or mercy) by the remission of the sins that are past. ....To him that is justified or forgiven, God will not impute sin' to his condemnation.... His sins, all his past sins, in thought, word and deed, are covered, are blotted out, shall not be remembered or mentioned against him, any more than if they had not been. God will not inflict on that sinner what he deserved to suffer, because the Son of his love hath suffered for him. And from that time we are accepted through the Beloved, reconciled to God through his blood, he loves and blesses and watches over us for good, even as if we had never sinned.[70]

---

[68] William Law, *The Grounds and Reasons of Christian Regeneration*, 1739.
[69] J. Wesley, *Works [BE]*, Vol. 3, pp.506, 507.
[70] J. Wesley, *Works [BE]*, Vol. 1, pp.189, 190.

John Wesley made justification the door to salvation; it is the first stage of Christian perfection. It is the first great change in the order of salvation and it is maintained by continual faith and obedience. If we are to understand Wesley clearly at this point, we must distinguish between justification and regeneration and between regeneration and entire sanctification.

John Wesley interpreted justification in a way significantly different than Martin Luther had done. Luther asserted that the sinner was justified when, through faith, the righteousness of Christ is imputed to him. This righteousness is the gift of God but it does not transform the sinner's inherent sinfulness. The justified man is declared just in Christ but he is still sinful and that old sinful nature will remain until death. Hence Luther's well-known dictum that the Christian is simul iustus et peccator, 'justified and yet still a sinner.'[71] John Calvin taught that true saving faith is given only to the elect and that faith enables the sinner to lay hold of the righteousness of God which is offered in the gospel. This righteousness is imputed to all true believers and it is accompanied by repentance and regeneration. This new life is also sanctification begun for, unlike Luther, Calvin insisted that the Christian believer will constantly strive to mortify the flesh, conquer his sinful nature and progress in holiness.[72] It was this understanding of Calvin's doctrine of justification implying the beginning of a transformation of the sinner's heart from sinfulness to holiness that

---

[71] See A.E. McGrath, *Christian Theology*, 1994, pp.382-391; see also, *Justification by Faith*, 1988, pp.48-61. Wesley wrote of Luther's understanding: 'Who hath wrote more ably than Martin Luther on justification by faith alone? And who was more ignorant of the doctrine of sanctification, or more confused, in his conceptions of this, of his total ignorance with regard to sanctification, there needs no more than to read over, without prejudice, his celebrated comment on the Epistle to the Galations,' *Works [BE]*, Vol. 3, p.505.

[72] R.N. Flew, *The Idea of Perfection in Christian Theology*, Chapter XII, The Reformation. There is a very full treatment of Calvin's understanding in R. Wallace, *Calvin's Doctrine of the Christian Life*, 1959, pp.313-332. For Calvin's view assessed from a Wesleyan viewpoint, see Paul M. Bassett, *Exploring Christian Holiness*, Vol. 2, The Historical Development, pp.164-177.

prompted Wesley to declare that in his understanding of justification he did not differ from Calvin's view by a hair's breadth.[73]

John Wesley did not teach that justification makes a man righteous. It declares him righteous on the basis of his faith in Christ's atonement. But at the same time, justification is accompanied by regeneration. To Wesley, justification and regeneration are concomitant but not identical. He defined regeneration in his 1760 sermon, *The New Birth*.

> That great change which God works in the soul, when he brings it into life; when he raises it from the death of sin to the life of righteousness. It is the change wrought in the whole soul by the Almighty Spirit of God, when it is created anew in Christ Jesus, when it is renewed after the image of God, in righteousness and true holiness, when the love of the world is changed into the love of God, pride in to humility, passion into meekness; hatred, envy, malice, into a sincere, tender, disinterested love for all mankind. In a word, it is that change whereby the earthly, sensual, devilish mind is turned into the mind which was in Christ. This is the nature of the new birth. 'So is everyone that is born of the Spirit.'[74]

This regeneration or conversion brings about a real, inward change in the soul. Believers in Christ, i.e., the regenerate, are 'so far perfect as not to commit sin,' that is, they do not continue to trespass God's law. Thus regeneration brings about a transformation in the Christian's life. While justification removes the guilt of sin, regeneration breaks the power of sin. In his 1748 sermon, *The Great Privilege of those that are Born of God*, Wesley spelled this out.

> Though it be allowed that justification and the new birth are, in point of time, inseparable from each other, yet are they easily distinguished, as being not the same, but things of a wholly different nature. Justification implies only a relative, the new birth a real, change. God in justifying us does something for us; in begetting us again he does the work in us.... The former changes our outward relation to God, so that of enemies we become children; by the latter our inmost souls are changed, so that of sinners we become saints. The one restores us to

---

[73] J. Wesley, *Letters*, Vol. 4, p.298.
[74] J. Wesley, *Works [BE]*, Vol. 2, pp.193, 194.

the favour, the other to the image, of God. The one is the taking away
the guilt, the other the taking away the power, of sin. So that although
they are joined together in point of time, yet are they of wholly distinct
natures.[75]

The regenerate or born again believer is in Wesley's understanding,
enabled by grace to overcome both inward and outward sin in the sense
that he does not go on wilfully sinning. Establishing this important
point will be sufficient answer to the charge often brought against
Wesley's teaching that he lowered the biblical standard of the new
birth in order to justify his doctrine of entire sanctification. Rather,
John Wesley had a high view of the nature of the new birth or
regeneration, teaching that it effected a radical change in the sinner and
was the beginning of a process of sanctification.

This work of regeneration in the sinner has been labelled 'initial
sanctification' by Wesleyan theologians.[76] This is not Wesley's own
language but it does describe fairly accurately his teaching. He did not
think that this initial sanctification was merely 'reckoning' the sinner
holy, nor was it some kind of imputed perfection. The regenerated
man is truly changed and he possesses a measure of holiness. In a 1745
polemic directed against what he believed to be the antinomian
tendencies of Moravian teaching, Wesley averred:

> Scriptural holiness is the image of God; the mind which was in Christ;
> the love of God and man; lowliness, gentleness, temperance, patience,
> chastity. And do you coolly affirm that this is only imputed to the
> believer, and that he has none at all of this holiness in him? Is
> temperance imputed only to him that is a drunkard still? or chastity to
> her that goes on in whoredom? Nay, but a believer is really chaste and
> temperate. And if so, he is thus holy in himself. Does a believer love
> God, or does he not? If he does, he has the love of God in him. Is he
> lowly, or meek, or patient at all? If he does, he has these tempers in
> himself; and if he has them not in himself, he is not lowly, or meek,
> or patient. You cannot therefore deny, that every believer has holiness

---

[75]   J. Wesley, *Works [BE]*, Vol. 1, pp.431, 432.
[76]   H.R. Dunning, *Grace, Faith and Holiness*, 1988, p.351.

in thought; else you deny, that he is holy at all, and if so, he cannot see the Lord.[77]

This holiness is not from the believer himself, i.e., he does not evince these graces by strenuous self-effort; instead they are wrought in him by the Spirit of God. He is inwardly changed and the graces of the Spirit thus become evident in his life. This is argued very clearly in Wesley's 1785 sermon, *On Working Out Our Own Salvation*. Having laid down that salvation begins with 'preventing grace,' Wesley goes on to show that it is continued by what he calls 'convincing grace.'

> Afterwards we experience the proper Christian salvation, whereby, through grace, we are saved by faith, consisting of those two grand branches, justification and sanctification. By justification we are saved from the guilt of sin; by sanctification we are saved from the power and root of sin, and restored to the image of God. All experience, as well as scripture, show this salvation to be both instantaneous and gradual. It begins the moment we are justified, in the holy, humble, gentle, patient love of God and man. It gradually increases from that moment till, in another instant, the heart is cleansed from all sin, and filled with pure love to God and man. But even that love increases more and more, till we grow up in all things into Him that is our Head; till we attain 'the measure of the stature of the fullness of Christ.'[78]

Wesley published this sermon in 1785, so it can be regarded as his mature thinking on the doctrine of salvation. A number of conclusions is evident from this extract.

1. Salvation is the gradual, increasing work of God in the sinner from the first movement of prevenient grace until final consummation in glory.

2. What Wesley terms 'proper Christian salvation' comes with repentance, when the sinner truly believes in Christ. It comprehends justification and regeneration; being cleared of the guilt of sin and having the power of sin broken in the human soul.

3. All this begins in a moment and it gradually increases.

---

[77] J. Wesley, *Works*, Vol. 10, p.203.
[78] J. Wesley, *Works [BE]*, Vol. 3, p.204.

4. There is another instance when the heart is fully cleansed from sin and filled with the love of God.

5. Beyond this cleansing and filling there is still the steady growth in grace and love.

Clearly for John Wesley his concept of scriptural holiness has two aspects. Negatively it concerns how God deals with sin in the believer. While regeneration frees the sinner from the guilt and power of sin; that is, sin understood as a transgression of the law; sanctification frees the regenerate from the in-being of sin; that is, sin understood as sinfulness and what Wesley often called 'the root' of sin. The regenerate Christian has experienced the dominion of sin broken in his life so that he is freed from its tyrannous control but he is still subject to indwelling sinfulness which Wesley often categorised as pride, anger, love of the world, self-will and unbelief. All these manifestations of the 'carnal mind' Wesley believed, were progressively dealt with in the work of sanctification and that work could be completed in this life, in that deliverance from all sin which he labelled 'entire sanctification.'

The other aspect of scriptural holiness is the positive one. It is the heart filled with the love of God and man; it is having 'all the mind that was in Christ;' it is walking 'even as Christ walked;' it is the image of God stamped on the heart; it is 'true righteousness and holiness.' It is the ongoing experience of the 'fruit of the Spirit' whereby love excludes sin and the entirely sanctified Christian is ever growing 'unto the measure of the stature of the fullness of Christ.' John Wesley's emphasis on the instantaneous character of entire sanctification was to occasion much criticism. Had he been content to preach and publish on scriptural holiness as the Christian's continual growth in grace he would probably have met very little opposition. But while the aspect of the obedient Christian's gradual and continual growth in holiness is everywhere prominent in John Wesley's writings, there is also the stress on the possibility of the instantaneous moment of entire sanctification.

If indeed he did think that entire sanctification, understood as cleansing from all inner sin, could be obtained instantaneously, that emphasis is not very prominent in his most important early writings on scriptural holiness. No mention of it is made in his 1741 sermon, *Christian Perfection,* or in either of his two important 1742 tracts, *The Character of a Methodist,* and, *The Principles of a Methodist.* Neither is it found in his 1743, *An Earnest Appeal to Men of Reason and Religion,* his 1745, *A Farther Appeal to Men of Reason and Religion,* nor yet in his 1746 letter, *The Principles of a Methodist farther Explained.* The earliest reference that can be found when Wesley clearly spoke of entire sanctification as an instantaneous blessing is his 1759 tract, *Thoughts on Christian Perfection.* This tract was occasioned by the mounting criticism that Wesley faced from antagonists who repudiated his alleged teaching as 'sinless perfection.' In the 1758 Conference the preachers, and especially the young preachers, were admonished not to speak of perfection too minutely or circumstantially, but rather in general and scriptural terms. Wesley's tract represented the clearest exposition he had yet given of this doctrine and he began with a definition. Christian Perfection is the loving God with all our heart, mind, soul and strength. This implies that no wrong temper, none contrary to love, remains in the soul and that all the thoughts, words and actions are governed by pure love. Wesley then poses the question: 'Is this death to sin and renewal in love gradual or instantaneous'? and gives the answer.

> A man may be dying for some time; yet he does not properly speaking die till the instant the soul is separated from the body. And in that instant he lives the life of eternity. In like manner he may be dying to sin for some time; yet he is not 'dead to sin' till sin is separated from the soul. And in that instant he lives the full love of love. And as the change undergone when the body dies is of a different kind, and infinitely greater that any we had known before, yea, such as till then it is impossible to conceive, so the change wrought when the soul dies to sin is of a different kind, and infinitely greater than any before, and that anyone can conceive till he experiences it. Yet he still grows in grace, in the knowledge of Christ, in the love and image of God, and will do so not only till death, but to all eternity. [79]

---

[79] J. Wesley, *Works,* Vol. 13, p.402.

From about the time this tract was published John Wesley's insistence on the instantaneous nature of entire sanctification becomes more noticeable in his sermons and publications. It is cogently argued for in his 1765 sermon, *The Scripture Way of Salvation,* and his 1766 treatise, *A Plain Account of Christian Perfection.* [80] With this frank admission that the Scriptures do not unequivocally support a doctrine of instantaneous entire sanctification, Wesley nevertheless urged that whether the work was gradual or instantaneous, the Christian should not rest until he is in the enjoyment of the blessing of scriptural holiness.

Given that admission, why had Wesley, on the other occasions, given such an emphasis to the instantaneous aspect of entire sanctification? The answer is – because of the testimonies he heard following what came to be known as the Otley Revival. Early in January 1760 about thirty members of the Methodist Society in Otley, Yorkshire, met together for prayer and mutual encouragement. A very strong sense of the presence of God gripped the gathering and fervent intercession, audible groanings and confessions of sin were mingled with loud praise and fervent testimonies. Some of those present found forgiveness of sin and others testified to a clear witness of being cleansed from all sin. There were similar scenes when the Society met again the following evening. This awakening spread quickly to other Methodist Societies and John Wesley closely investigated the phenomena. Years later he wrote of it:

> Before they parted, three believed God had fulfilled His word, and cleansed them from all unrighteousness. The next evening they met again, and the Lord was again present to heal the broken in heart. One received remission from all sin, and three more believed God had cleansed them from all sin.... Here began that glorious work of sanctification, which had been nearly at a stand for twenty years. But from time to time it spread, first through various parts of Yorkshire, afterwards in London, then through most parts of England; next through Dublin, Limerick, and all the south and west of Ireland. And wherever the work of sanctification increased, the whole work of God increased in all its branches. Many were convinced of sin, many

---

[80]   J. Wesley, *Works [BE]*, Vol. 2, pp.155-169.

justified, many backsliders healed. So it was in the London Society in particular. In February, 1761, it contained upwards of three-and-twenty hundred members; in 1763, above eight-and-twenty hundred.[81]

The revival that began at Otley continued for some two or three years and one of its prominent manifestations was the number of Methodists who sought, and testified to have found, entire sanctification from all sin in an instantaneous experience of God's sanctifying grace· In the Bristol Society there was a large increase in attendance and much sincere seeking after God. Wesley wrote of it that it seems that God was pleased to pour out His spirit this year, on every part both of England and Ireland, in a manner we had never seen before. In Dublin he questioned more than forty members who were professing 'the pure love of God.' At Manchester he found some sixty members 'who believed God had cleansed their hearts.' So widespread was this revival among the Methodist Societies and so convincing the evidence Wesley found of it, that he spoke of it as Methodism's 'day of Pentecost.' Although a small number of professors later fell away, yet such was the depth and permanence of this revival that he spoke of it as 'the great work of God.... the greatest, I believe, that has been wrought in Europe since the Reformation.'[82]

Many years later John Wesley gave evidence of how he had taken time to question many of those who testified to an experience of instantaneous entire sanctification in the wake of the Otley Revival. In London he had 'carefully examined' six hundred and fifty two professors of scriptural holiness and of their testimonies he concluded he could 'see no reason to doubt.' The same experience of an instantaneous cleansing from inner sin had come to many believers all over the country and not one had testified to gradual sanctification. Wesley concluded:

> And every one of these (after the most careful enquiry I have not found one exception either in Great Britain or Ireland) has declared that his deliverance from sin was instantaneous, that the change was

---

[81]   J .Wesley, *Works*, Vol. 13, p.350.
[82]   J. Wesley, *Works*, Vol. 13, p.355.

wrought in a moment. Had half of these, or one third, or one in twenty, declared that it was gradually wrought in them, I should have believed this, with regard to them, and thought that some were gradually sanctified and some instantaneously. But as I have not found, in so long a space of time, a single person speaking thus; as all who believe they are sanctified, declare with one voice, that the change was wrought in a moment, I cannot but believe that sanctification is commonly, if not always, an instantaneous work.[83]

Did John Wesley, then, press this point of instantaneousness as a result of examining the experiences of those who testified to entire sanctification rather than finding it explicitly taught in Scripture? The answer must be yes. The evidence shows that during and after the revival that began in Otley, John Wesley found a significant increase in the number of those who readily testified to their experience of scriptural holiness, and, furthermore, they also bore witness to an instantaneous blessing in their souls. Wesley was also further convinced that stressing the instantaneousness nature of entire sanctification was a certain means of promoting gradual sanctification and furthering the whole work of God. The following extract from the Minutes of the 1768 Conference is one of Wesley's most definitive paragraphs on the point.

> You are all agreed that we may be saved from all sin before death. The substance then, is settled, but as to the circumstances, is the change gradual or instantaneous? It is both the one and the other. From the moment we are justified, there may be a gradual sanctification, or growing in grace, daily advance in the knowledge and love of God. And if sin cease before death, there must in the nature of the thing, be an instantaneous change; there must be a last moment wherein it does exist, and a first moment wherein it does not.... Certainly we must insist on the gradual change, and that earnestly and continually. And are there not reasons why we should insist on the instantaneous also? If there be such a blessed change before death, should we not encourage all believers to expect it? and the rather, because constant experience shows, the more earnestly they expect this, the more swiftly and steadily does the gradual work of God go on in their soul; the more watchful they are against all sin, the more careful to grow in

---

[83]   J. Wesley, *Works [BE]*, Vol. 3, p.178.

grace, the more zealous of good works, and the more punctual in their attendance on all the ordinances of God. Whereas, just the contrary effects are observed whenever this expectation ceases. Therefore whoever would advance the gradual change in believers, should strongly insist on the instantaneous.[84]

As with justification, sanctification, both gradual and entire, is received by faith. Because it is by faith, Wesley stressed that therefore it is within reach of all. As a benefit of the Atonement it is the privilege of all believers and all Christians should strive for it. But John Wesley was careful to stress that the attainment of this experience of entire cleansing from all sin in this present life was not a condition of final salvation. It should be remembered that Wesley did not affirm that all who do not walk in this way are on the high road to hell. He went on to say that those who walk in the lower way will find mercy 'in the close of life, through the blood of the covenant.' However, Christian perfection is the higher way and is within the reach of every Christian.

Having looked at how Wesley understood scriptural holiness in terms of the whole work of salvation, and his insistence that it is the goal to which every believer in Christ is called, it will be useful to look at how he defined this blessing. Scattered throughout John Wesley's writings, and especially in his letters, there are many statements on the nature of scriptural holiness. Many different terms are used to describe it but more and more Wesley came to see that the focus is love, love to God and man. At the first Conference in 1744 the question was raised: 'What is implied in being made perfect in love?' The answer given was: 'The loving the Lord our God with all our heart and with our mind, and soul, and strength.'[85] Writing from Birmingham, on June 22, 1763, to Henry Venn, he declared that justification and holiness were his only points.

> If any one will convince me of my errors, I will heartily thank him. I believe all the Bible as far as I understand it, and am ready to be convinced. If I am an heretic, I became such by reading the Bible. All my nothings I draw from thence.... unless in the single point of

---

[84] J. Wesley, *Works [BE]*, Vol. 10, pp.363, 364.
[85] J. Wesley, *Works [BE]*, Vol. 10, p.132.

Justification by Faith.... What I want is holiness of heart and life....
'But you hold Perfection.' True – that is, loving God with all our heart,
and serving Him with all our strength. I teach nothing more, nothing
less than this.[86]

Three years later he wrote to Mrs Elizabeth Bennis, saying that 'the
highest degree of holiness.... is no other than pure love, an heart
devoted to God, one design and one desire.'[87] Later that year he wrote
his *Plain Account* and in one memorable paragraph he portrayed love
as the very zenith of all Christian experience.

> Love is the highest gift of God; humble, gentle, patient love.... All
> visions, revelations, manifestations whatever, are little things
> compared to love.... There is nothing higher in religion; there is, in
> effect, nothing else; if you look for anything but more love, you are
> looking wide of the mark, you are getting out of the royal way. And
> when you are asking others, 'Have you received this or that blessing?'
> if you mean anything but more love, you mean wrong.... Settle it then
> in your heart, that from the moment God has saved you from all sin,
> you are to aim at nothing more, but more of that love described in the
> thirteenth of Corinthians. You can go no higher than this, till you are
> carried into Abraham's bosom.[88]

In 1771 he wrote to Walter Churchey, a Welsh lawyer and a keen
Methodist. 'Entire sanctification, or Christian perfection, is nothing
more nor less than pure love, love expelling sin and governing both the
heart and life of a child of God. The Refiner's fire purges out all that
is contrary to love, and that many times by a pleasing smart. Leave all
this to Him that does all things well and that loves you better than you
do yourself.' [89] One of John Wesley's more regular correspondents
was Miss Hannah Ball of High Wycombe who was to be the pioneer
of Sunday Schools in Methodism. When she asked if special
revelations were part of the experience of scriptural holiness, Wesley
replied:

---

[86]   J. Wesley, *Letters*, Vol. 4, p.216.
[87]   J. Wesley, *Letters*, Vol. 5, p.6.
[88]   J. Wesley, *Works*, Vol. 11, p.430.
[89]   J. Wesley, *Letters*, Vol. 5, p.223.

I have lately made diligent inquiry into the experience of many that are perfected in love. And I find a very few of them who have a clear revelation of the several Persons in the ever-blessed Trinity. It therefore appears that this is by no means essential to Christian perfection. All that is necessarily implied therein is humble, gentle, patient love; love regulating all the tempers, and governing all the words and actions.[90]

While this understanding that love is the essence of scriptural holiness is found in John Wesley's writings from the beginning of his itinerant ministry, the emphasis becomes more marked from the 1760s onwards. Many scholars who have analysed John Wesley's doctrine of scriptural holiness have done so using only a hermeneutic of sinlessness. It is clear enough that evidence for such a hermeneutic abounds in Wesley's writings for he never tired of reiterating that salvation, in all its stages, is salvation from sin. But it is the contention of this Lecture that there is even more evidence for another hermeneutic by which to understand Wesley's 'grand depositum' – a hermeneutic of love. The quotations already given point in this direction and in the final years of Wesley's life and ministry this focus on love as the *summum bonum* becomes more and more apparent.

Three sermons from the last decade of his life amply illustrate this point. Early in 1784 Wesley published in his *Arminian Magazine* a sermon based on James 1:4, 'Let patience have its perfect work.' The title, 'On Patience,' was something of a misnomer for the sermon's main theme was scriptural holiness. The perfect work of patience is nothing less than 'the perfect love of God.' This is the whole of religion, it is the whole mind that was in Christ, it is nothing less than the renewal of the soul in the image of God. Such is the great change wrought in the soul by justification that entire sanctification is not 'any new kind of holiness;' rather it is a marked increase in our experience of the love of God.

From the moment we are justified till we give up our spirits to God, love is the fulfilling of the law - of the whole evangelical law, which

---

[90] J. Wesley, *Letters*, Vol. 6, p.266.

took place of the Adamic law when the first promise of the seed of the woman was made. Love is the sum of Christian sanctification, only in various degrees, in the believers by St. John into 'little children, young men, and fathers.'.... But it may be inquired, In what manner does God work this entire, this universal change in the soul of the believer?.... But I have not found in so long a space of time a single person speaking thus - as all who believe they are sanctified declare with one voice that the change was wrought in a moment - I cannot but believe the sanctification is commonly, if not always, an instantaneous work.[91]

Wesley could not be more unambiguous in declaring that the various levels of Christian experience are but various levels of the experience of the love of God in the soul. It is begun in regeneration and as the Christian grows in faith and holiness, he increases in love, in 'every part of the image of God,' until, 'thoroughly convinced of inbred sin,' it pleases God to 'purify his heart and cleanse him from all unrighteousness.' Now his heart is filled with the love of God, and Wesley describes the evidence, as, *On The Wedding Garment.*

The righteousness of Christ is, doubtless, necessary for any soul that enters into glory. But so is personal holiness, too, for every child of man.... But it is highly needful to be observed that they are necessary in different respects. The former is necessary to entitle us to heaven; the latter, to qualify us for it. Without the righteousness of Christ we could have no claim to glory; without holiness we could have no fitness for it. By the former we become members of Christ, children of God, and heirs of the kingdom of heaven. By the latter we are 'made meet to be partakers of the inheritance of the saith in light.'.... Such has been my judgment for these threescore years, without any material alteration. Only about fifty years ago I had a clearer view than before of justification by faith; and in this from that very hour I have varied, no not an hair's breath.... The sum of all this is: the God of love is willing to save all the souls that he has made. This he has proclaimed to them in his Word, together with the terms of salvation revealed by the Son of his love, who gave his own life that they believe in him might have everlasting life.... Choose holiness by my grace, which is the way, the only way, to everlasting life.... Be holy, and be

---

[91] J. Wesley, *Works [BE]*, Vol. 3, pp.174-178.

happy; happy in this world, and happy in the world to come. 'Holiness becometh his house for ever!'[92]

In December 1784 Wesley published his sermon, *On Perfection,* a sermon in tone and emphasis quite significantly different from his 1741 sermon, *Christian Perfection.* Thomas Oden, one of the most distinguished contemporary Wesley scholars, labels this sermon 'the most penetrating precis of Wesley's matured doctrine of perfection.'[93] The old distinctions are there as before, showing that Christian perfection is neither Adamic or angelic. But scriptural holiness is more than perfectionism understood as deliverance from all sin, outward and inward; it is the whole heart filled with the love of God.

> What is then the perfection of which man is capable while he dwells in a corruptible body? It is the complying with that kind command, 'My son, give me thy heart.' It is the 'loving the Lord his God with all his heart, and with all his soul, and with all his mind.' This is the sum of Christian perfection; it is all comprised in that one word, love. The first branch of it is the love of God: and as he that loves God loves his brother also, it is inseparably connected with the second, 'Thou shalt love thy neighbour as thyself.' Thou shalt love every man as thy own soul, as Christ loved us.[94]

John Wesley had not retracted his lifelong emphasis on holiness as salvation from all sin. Jesus still saves his people, the sermon argues, from their sins, 'the root as well as the branches.' But now that deliverance is described as 'the least, the lowest branch [of perfection],

---

[92] J. Wesley, *Works [BE],* Vol. 4, pp.144-148.
[93] Thomas C. Oden, *John Wesley's Scriptural Christianity,* 1994, p.323.
[94] J. Wesley, *Works [BE],* Vol. 3, p.74. There is a very fine treatment of John Wesley's understanding of scriptural holiness in terms of love made perfect in Mildred Bangs Wynkoop, *A Theology of Love: The Dynamic of Wesleyanism,* 1972. In her chapter, 'A Hermeneutical Approach to Wesley,' she writes: 'The summarising word was Wesley's ultimate hermeneutic is love. Every strand in his thought, the warm heart of every doctrine, the passion of every sermon, the test of every claim to Christian grace, was love. So central is love that to be 'Wesleyan' is to be committed to a theology of love,' p.101. A somewhat similar argument is advanced in Harald Lindstrom's, *Wesley and Sanctification,* 1950, especially Chapter 5, 'Christian Love.'

only the negative part of the great salvation.'[95] Holiness is the love of God and man, it is the mind that was in Christ, it is 'the one undivided fruit of the Spirit,' being 'inwardly conformed to the whole image and will of God.' After the years of argument, controversy and misunderstanding that accompanied Wesley's exposition of scriptural holiness, now in the final years of his ministry there was a clearer vision of what Albert Outler rightly called the 'doctrine's proper focus.'[96]

Across a period of fifty years John Wesley did not vary significantly in his understanding of Christian holiness, though notice must be taken of the nuances of the later years. In such a prolific writer it would be surprising if there were not some statements seemingly at odds with others, but John Wesley's half century of teaching on scriptural holiness is remarkably free, in the main, of inconsistencies and contradictions. He was convinced that this ideal of the holy life was in the Bible and that settled the dispute. There were times when the pressures on him, occasioned by the lack of fruit among those who professed entire sanctification and by the hostilities of those evangelical Christians who strongly opposed his teaching, forced him, as in June 1768, to write to his brother Charles, almost in despair, and ask: 'Shall we go on in asserting perfection against all the world? Or shall we quietly let it drop?'[97] But he did not let it drop because in spite of all the distractions both from within and without the Methodist Societies, he was sure this teaching was found in Scripture. The greatest contribution made by Wesleyan theology to the Christian Church is undoubtedly its teaching on Christian holiness, reinforced by the hymns of Charles Wesley dealing with scriptural holiness in all its many facets.

John Wesley took up the Reformers' doctrine of justification by faith and developed it along New Testament lines to the fuller doctrine of sanctification by faith. We may not agree with every single conclusion

---

[95] J. Wesley, *Works [BE]*, Vol. 3, p.76.
[96] A. Outler, 'An Introductory Comment,' *Works [BE]*, p.70.
[97] J. Wesley, *Letters*, Vol. 5, p.93.

that Wesley came to, nor with his precise interpretation of every passage of scripture, yet it can be asserted that John Wesley had sound exegetical grounds for his main conclusions concerning the great salvation. There have been many critical studies of Wesley's teaching on scriptural holiness, from within and without Wesleyanism, yet one remarkable fact emerges; after two centuries of close analysis and investigation no one has been able to demonstrate that Wesley was in error in his main contentions. This is surely a most significant conclusion; John Wesley's delineation of New Testament holiness has survived every challenge. As William Sangster argued: 'As we have surveyed Wesley's textual foundations, we have noticed the shadows of dubiety cast by scholarship on a translation, or interpretation, here and there, but for the most part, the stones stand.'[98]

In conclusion it is important that we ask ourselves today. What is the contemporary significance of John Wesley's understanding of Scriptural holiness? In particular how should all those who want to be designated 'Wesleyan' respond to it? What is our reaction to the grand depositum?

1. If we are convinced that this distinctive reflects New Testament teaching, then it must have its place, both in our own personal spiritual quest and in our teaching and preaching ministries. One of the most important scholarly works ever written in this area was Newton Flew's, *The Idea of Perfection in Christian Theology*. Flew's masterly summary began with the teaching of Jesus and ended with an appraisal of the views of Peter Forsyth. Throughout his chapters of historical investigation Flew was seeking to answer the double question raised in his 'Introduction;' What is the Christian ideal for the present life?, and is it the will of God that by his grace we should attain to it? Almost four hundred pages later Flew answered these questions:

> The doctrine of Christian perfection, understood not as an assertion that a final attainment of the goal of the Christian life is possible in this world, but as a declaration that a supernatural destiny, a relative attainment of the goal which does not exclude growth, is the will of

---

[98]   W.E. Sangster, *The Path to Perfection*, 1943, p.52.

God for us in this world and is attainable lies not merely upon the bypath of Christian theology, but upon the high road.[99]

We need not fear that the Wesleyan doctrine of perfect love is some kind of Pietistic deviation or revivalist provincialism. It is scripture's 'highway of holiness', what Flew called 'the high road,' and what John Wesley so often called 'the great salvation.' We are more likely to give it too little attention than too much. In modern terminology this doctrine is part of the New Testament kerygma, therefore we can rightly label it 'scriptural holiness.'

2. The climate in modern Evangelicalism is right for a new emphasis on purity of heart, the 'faith that works by love.' The last three decades have seen a veritable tide of literature on the work of the Spirit, especially His indwelling the believer and His ministry in the Church as the body of Christ. Without feeling at all in any sense superior, the student of John Wesley's life and theology can hardly refrain from at least a slight smile when he hears of these so called new discoveries about the Spirit filled life. His reply is that they are hardly new; they have been part of the heritage of authentic Wesleyanism for two centuries. The accent on spirituality and spiritual power is one that the Wesleyan Christian will gladly welcome. He doesn't claim that John Wesley said the last word on this, or indeed on any other scriptural doctrine, but he does believe that Wesley laid down scriptural guidelines that are as relevant today as when he published his *Plain Account*.

John Wesley's emphasis on entire sanctification being inward holiness, the love of God and neighbour, the likeness of Christ stamped on the heart, finds welcome in our day. Colin Urquhart, a recognised leader and writer in what is broadly called the Charismatic Movement, complains in his book, *Holy Fire*, that in spite of all the attention that has been given to the administrations and gifts of the Spirit, there is a sad lack of emphasis on the fundamental of holiness.[100] And it is

---

[99] R.N. Flew, *The Idea of Perfection in Christian Theology*, p.390.
[100] C. Urquhart, *Holy Fire*, 1984, Chapters 6 and 14.

precisely here that John Wesley's 'distinctive' has so much to offer the modern Church. As a 19th century hymn writer expressed it, holiness of heart is the goal of all Christian experience and pilgrimage:

> Blest are the pure in heart
> For they shall see our God
> The secret of the Lord is theirs
> Their soul is Christ's abode.
>
> He to the lowly soul
> Doth still Himself impart
> And for His dwelling and His throne
> Chooseth the pure in heart.[101]

3. There is one other area where John Wesley's doctrine of scriptural holiness challenges us today and that is with regards to evangelism. The recognition of that challenge surely has an appropriate place in a Lecture that memorialises the life and ministry of Maynard James. For half a century John Wesley travelled, preached, wrote, published, organised his Societies, and inspired his converts to call the nation back to God and God blessed his labours with signal success. Do we need even to ask the question if there was a connection between his unceasing evangelistic labours and his doctrine of love for God and man? Surely we have the right to be at least a little impatient with those critics who go through John Wesley's writings with a fine comb, looking for some passage where Wesley gives personal testimony to entire sanctification using certain terminology and usually concluding that because they cannot find precisely what they expected him to say, therefore it must be conceded that he never gave personal testimony to his own distinctive doctrine. Quite simply these critics are looking for the wrong thing in the wrong place. The quality of John Wesley's personal life, the evidence of those who knew him best, his complete dedication to God and His work, and his unswerving devotion to saving souls for half a century, these are the 'proofs' that the

---

[101] J. Keble, *The Methodist Hymn Book*, 1933, p.950.

distinctive doctrine he inculcated so strongly found abundant manifestation in his own life.

As we face the challenge of evangelism in post-Christian and multi-faith Britain, John Wesley's theology is neither irrelevant or redundant. Scriptural holiness, understood as love to God and man, makes every Christian an evangelist; the 'warmed heart' is, in Charles Wesley's lines, 'full of Christ, and longs its glorious matter to declare.'[102] So in 21st century Britain, as in 18th century, the fervent prayer of every Christian, and certainly of every Wesleyan Christian, ought to be:

> That I Thy mercy may proclaim
> That all mankind Thy truth may see
> Hallow Thy great and glorious Name
> And perfect holiness in me.[103]

---

[102] G. Osborn, *The Poetical Works of John and Charles Wesley*, 13 Vols., Vol. 8, p.103.
[103] G. Osborn, *The Poetical Works of John and Charles Wesley*, 13 Vols., Vol. 2, p.319.

JOHN WESLEY –
PROTAGONIST OF THE CATHOLIC SPIRIT

When John Wesley published his sermon, *The Catholic Spirit*, in 1755, it was much more than merely an addition to his sermon corpus. In content and intention, it expressed Wesley's understanding of what the essentials of Christian experience are, and his resolve to work with all those who honoured Christ and promoted his kingdom, even if he differed from them in some doctrinal matters. Earlier he had published another sermon along similar lines, *A Caution Against Bigotry*. In both sermons Wesley spelt out his warning against the sectarian spirit that divides the people of God and prevents Christians from understanding that God is present and working in fellowships and parties and denominations other than their own. In this essay that proclaims a true ecumenist of spirit and acceptance without sacrificing orthodox and evangelical truths, John Wesley has something to say to all of us in the 21st century. We shall see what Wesley meant by the catholic spirit and how he practised that spirit in half a century of preaching, writing and setting up the Methodist Societies.

The sermon on bigotry is based on Mark 9:38, 39, where Jesus cautioned his disciples not to exclude the man casting out demons just because he did not belong to the circle of the Jesus' disciples. Wesley defined bigotry as 'too strong an attachment to, or fondness for, our own party, opinion, Church, and religion.'[104] The reference to casting out demons is taken to mean the proclamation of the gospel in the widest sense. The devil has set up his throne in every human heart and it only the power of Christ, mediated in the gospel, that can evict him. Wesley here assumes a very orthodox understanding of original sin and the deep conviction that the gospel is God's power for our salvation. So the man casting out demons represents all those who truly and faithfully proclaim Christ's gospel. But how, Wesley asks, will we recognise such a man? The test is really quite simple. Have we sufficient proof of a particular man or woman, now unquestionably a

---

[104] J. Wesley, *Works [BE]*, Vol. 11, p.76.

Christian, and who was previously a 'gross, open sinner'? If there is also plain proof that this transformation of life came about by hearing a particular preacher, then that preacher unquestionably casts out demons. The point that Wesley wants to make is clear enough – such a preacher is exercising a gospel ministry and we should not hinder him. Having detailed the various ways in which Christians hinder one another because of bigotry, Wesley goes much further. It is not enough merely to tolerate the other preacher and refrain from attacking his methods and party and his particular theological stance; we must positively pray for him and speak well of his ministry. The sermon concludes with a very moving exordium.

> If you will avoid all bigotry, acknowledge the finger of God. And not only acknowledge but rejoice in his work, and praise his name with thanksgiving…. Speak well of him wheresoever you are; defend his character and his mission. Enlarge as far as you can his sphere of action. Show him all kindness in word and deed. And cease not to cry to God on his behalf, that he may save both himself and them that hear him.[105]

Most of us will probably have to conclude, to our shame, that there have been too many occasions in the work of God when we have not treated colleagues and our brethren in the Lord in the way Wesley recommends.

A few years later John Wesley published his sermon, *The Catholic Spirit*. He based it on Jehu's question to Jehonadab; 'Is thine heart right, as my heart is with thy heart?' And Jehonadab answered: 'It is. If it be, give me thine hand.'[106] While acknowledging that Jehu was not exactly a model saint, yet Wesley urges that his example here is one that every Christian should imitate. Jehu's question is not about Jehonadab's opinions but about his spirit, his attitude and his affections. How does he regard his neighbour? In a word, is there love in his heart? And then Wesley writes a glorious sentence, pleading that even allowing our difference of opinions, we must not let this stand in

---

[105] J. Wesley, *Works [BE]*, Vol. 11, p.77.
[106] 2 Kings 10:15.

the way of brotherly affection. 'Though we can't think alike, may we not love alike?'[107] John Wesley wrote much in defence of that understanding of Christian sanctification that he understood as love perfected, and this sentence is as good a practical summary of it as anything he argued elsewhere.

Wesley's sermon goes on to explain that while Christians have differing modes of public worship, differing ideas about church government and differing practices about the subjects and manner of baptism, yet far more important than any of these is the question: do we love God and all mankind? If we do, then, says Wesley, give me your hand, and I will seek, by God's grace, to love you in His name. This 'catholic spirit' is more important than denominational zeal, or distinctives or any of the outward characteristics of the various 'parties' that make up Christ's Church. Where it is found, Christians go forward in God's work hand in hand, and the One great Head of the Church is glorified in his people.

Like the sermon against bigotry, this sermon is a call to Christians to put away the party spirit, the unkind criticism, the harsh judgements and the censorious back-biting that Wesley knew only too well to be so prevalent in his own day. The first decade of the revival had witnessed not only strong opposition from many of the clergy of the established church, but bitter controversy inside 'Methodism' itself. Hardly had Wesley's 'field preaching' begun in Bristol in 1739 when the 'Societies' of the converts were sharply divided over the doctrines of election and predestination. The long-standing friendship begun at Oxford between John and Charles Wesley and George Whitefield was strained to breaking point. There were rival claims about who really 'owned' the revival work in Bristol and allegations that John Wesley had usurped Whitefield's rightful leadership. Back in London the Moravians and the 'Methodists' were going separate ways, and the split among the members of the Fetter Lane Society epitomised the

---

[107] J. Wesley, *Works [BE]*, Vol. 11, p.82.

growing divide among these former good friends.[108] All these sad divisions, with the accompanying rancour and mutual suspicion, must have been in Wesley's mind when he published this sermon. If only Christians would love one another as their Lord had directed them! There was a great need to call fellow-believers back to the catholic spirit and that was the sermon's intention.

John Wesley knew that however well-intentioned this sermon was, its plea to 'think and let think'[109] could easily be misunderstood for theological and doctrinal indifference. The sermon concluded with a rejection of what Wesley called 'speculative latitudinarianism.' This meant uncertainty and indifference about the doctrines of the historic Christian faith. Wesley protested that the man of true catholic spirit is as 'fixed as the sun in his judgement concerning the main branches of Christian doctrine.' Among those who subscribed to the Creeds of the Church there had always been differences of opinion about ecclesiastical practices and those doctrines that did not directly affect our salvation. With many of high-Calvinist persuasion, Wesley did not share their opinions about absolute predestination, limited atonement and irresistible grace. Against Roman Catholic theologians John Wesley had no place for their teachings on papal infallibility, a propitiatory Mass, the adoration of Mary, purgatory and other Roman doctrines. But with protagonists of both Calvinistic and Catholic Christianity, Wesley, while rejecting what he saw as their peripheral teachings, was at one in confessing with them such foundation doctrines as the holy Trinity, the deity of Christ, original sin, justification by faith, holy living and final destiny. But this catholic spirit, that strongly identified with all who asserted the historic doctrines of the faith, was not at all complacent about dangerous diversions. This was well illustrated in Wesley's response to what he

---

[108] The origins and characteristics of the Fetter Lane Society are discussed in C. Podmore, *The Moravian Church in England, 1728-1760*, Oxford: Clarendon Press, 1998, pp.29-71.

[109] In his 1742 apologetic, The Character of a Methodist, Wesley wrote: 'As to all opinions, which do not strike at the root of Christianity, we "think and let think."' J. Wesley, *Works [BE]*, Vol. 9, p.34.

saw as the reductionist Christology of John Taylor of Norwich. A popular Socinian preacher and writer, Taylor published his book, *The Scripture Doctrine of Original Sin, Proposed to Free and Candid Examination*. Written in a lively and very readable style and showing a mastery of the Biblical languages, it was the 18th century's most trenchant attack on the orthodox doctrine of original sin. As a corollary, it undermined the evangelical teaching on justification by faith and, as a pronounced Socinian, Taylor saw Christ as the world's greatest teacher and exemplar of God's grace but not as God incarnate.

As John Wesley itinerated across the four kingdoms of Great Britain, he lamented that Taylor's teaching was producing disciples who ridiculed evangelical Christianity.[110] He waited for some orthodox theologian to reply to Taylor, and when none appeared, Wesley took up the cudgels. Retiring for some ten weeks to a friend's house in London late in 1756, he wrote, *The Scripture Doctrine of Original Sin according to Scripture, Reason and Experience*. Running to some 522 quarto pages, it was the single longest treatise that Wesley published. It was followed two years later by a summary, in his sermon, *On Original Sin*, and there were letters to friends about this controversy, including a letter to Taylor himself. In all these publications Wesley did not attack Taylor in person; indeed he acknowledged that he esteemed his opponent a man of 'uncommon sense and knowledge.' But Wesley had no time for Taylor's Enlightenment optimism about fallen mankind. No writer since Mahomet had given such a wound to Christianity.[111] Wesley unsheathed his controversial sword and threw away the scabbard. What was at stake was nothing less than our 'eternal peace.' The issue between himself and Taylor was, quite simply, 'Christianity or heathenism.' Either he had mistaken the whole of Christianity from beginning to end – or Taylor had. Wesley's

---

[110] In his *Journal* for Sunday August 28, 1748, Wesley records his visit to Shackerley in Lancashire: 'Abundance of people were gathered before six, many of whom were disciples of Dr. Taylor, laughing at Original Sin, and, consequently, at the whole frame of scriptural Christianity.' Wesley, *Works [BE]*, Vol. 20, pp.245, 246.

[111] J. Wesley, *Letters*, Vol. 4, p.67.

scheme – or Taylor's – was as 'contrary to the scriptural as the Koran is.' If the scriptural doctrines of redemption, justification and the new birth are removed, or, alternatively, explained as Taylor explains them, then Christianity is no better than heathenism. If the doctrine of Original Sin means no more than John Taylor asserts, then Christianity is merely a system of good advice and the religion of St Paul has no pre-eminence over the teaching of Socrates or Epictetus.[112]

Having looked at John Wesley's plea for the Catholic spirit to prevail among Christians, and noting that it did not mean indifference to plausible heresies, it is time to turn and see how far Wesley exemplified this spirit in his own life and work and ministry. An appropriate starting point is the year 1739 when Wesley first organised his followers into 'Societies.' Most of these men and women had been awakened by the Methodist preachers and they requested Wesley to help them in discipleship. In this way the Societies were begun and the conditions of membership were simple: a desire to 'flee from the wrath to come and to save their souls.'[113] The rules of these Societies forbade, among other things, swearing, Sabbath-breaking, drunkenness and quarrelling. There were also positive injunctions to doing good, attending the means of grace, studying Scripture and family and private prayer. But John Wesley imposed no doctrinal or theological test on those joining the Societies. They might be Calvinists or Catholics, Presbyterians or Moravians, Quakers or Dissenters of any colour – all this made no difference.[114] If their intention was to seek the salvation of their souls, then they were welcome in Wesley's Societies. Whatever opinions they held about other doctrines, provided these were not the occasion of conflict and controversy, Wesley made them welcome. With the help of his preachers and assistants and class-leaders, he watched over their souls, preached, taught and explained repentance and faith and then instructed the regenerate to grow in the love of God and man.

---

[112] J. Wesley, *Letters*, Vol. 4, p.67.
[113] J. Wesley, *Works [BE]*, Vol. 9, p.70.
[114] J. Wesley, *Letters*, Vol. 4, pp.297, 298.

In a famous passage he said of himself that in life he wanted to know one thing – 'the way to heaven.'[115] Having found it, he spent the rest of his life helping others to find it. Salvation was not in creeds, or dogmas, or styles of worship, or denominational labels but through faith in the Son of God. Taking the world as his parish,[116] he laboured to help men and women on the way to heaven, for the catholic spirit permitted no barriers among those who practised the love of God and man.

John Wesley's 'United Societies,' as they were first called, had been preceded by the Religious Societies. These had come into existence in the late 17th century, mostly as the work of Dr Antony Horneck.[117] They, too, catered for those who wanted gatherings where prayer, fellowship and devotion reading were encouraged. But they catered mostly for a religious elite and offered little attraction to those who were not regular worshippers or acquainted with religious matters. In contrast, Wesley's Societies were almost democratic, and their pattern ensured that they were geared to help those who were mostly strangers to religious practices, forms and terminology. Indeed many of these early 'Methodists' were illiterate and the Societies introduced them not only to the essentials of Christian doctrine but also spurred them to learn to read and write.

In the late 1730s and early 40s, the Methodists were divided by wrangles over election and predestination. An anonymous letter circulated among the converts in Bristol, warning them not to listen to John Wesley because he preached against predestination. Although the accusation was false, the rumours spread and finally Wesley preached, and then published his sermon, *Free Grace*. It was a strong attack on absolute predestination but no names were mentioned.

---

[115] J. Wesley, *Works [BE]*, pp.104-106.
[116] J. Wesley, *Works [BE]*, Vol. 25, p.616.
[117] Antony Horneck (1641-97) came to England from Bacharach in Germany in 1661. In about 1678 he began to organise meetings for young men in and around London in order that they 'might apply themselves to good discourse and to things wherein they might edify one another.' See J.S. Simon, *John Wesley and the Religious Societies*, London, Epworth Press, 1921, p.10.

George Whitefield replied with his, *A Letter to the Rev. Mr John Wesley*, censuring him for publishing a provocative sermon and attacking Wesley's theology. The outcome of this doctrinal quarrel among former friends was that the revival split into two groups; those who followed the Wesley brothers were designated Wesleyan Methodists and those who sided with Whitefield and his supporters became known as Calvinistic Methodists. This 'parting of the ways' among old friends hurt both parties and it bred mistrust and suspicion of fellow believers on both sides.

The record of this early, and lasting, breach in the work of the 18th century revival constitutes a sad and depressing chapter. While this historic divide, usually but inaccurately, labelled the Calvinistic/Arminian dispute, had been part of Evangelicalism since the 17th century, its resurrection among the 18th century Methodists can never be an occasion of rejoicing for the evangelical historian or theologian. Former friends went their separate ways, fellowships were broken off, misunderstandings and half-truths proliferated and the work of God and evangelism suffered. If only John Wesley and George Whitefield had come together and, even if complete doctrinal agreement was not possible, surely there could have been a brotherly rapport that eclipsed discord and allowed the glorious work of soul-saving to prosper. Looking at both camps, with Whitefield, John Cennick and their supporters on one side, and the Wesley brothers and their preachers on the other, what potential there was to advance the work of God. What might have been achieved if these good and godly people had been catholic enough in spirit to agree to disagree on some theological interpretations in order to support each other in evangelising the land.

Writing to Whitefield in the midst of the warfare, John Wesley acknowledged that it was bigotry that divided the Evangelicals.

> The case is quite plain. There are bigots both for Predestination and against it. God is sending a message to those on either side. But neither will receive it, unless from one of his own opinion. Therefore for a time you are suffered to be of one opinion and I of another. But

when His time is come God will do what man cannot - namely, make us both of one mind. [118]

Over the next few years this dispute rumbled on and there was also a gap opening up between John Wesley and the Moravians. Ever since he had first met the Moravians on a voyage to America in 1735, John Wesley had been profoundly influenced by their teaching and example of holy living. His ties with them in Georgia were very strong, and when he returned to England early in 1738, he and Charles formed a close friendship with the Moravian Peter Bohler. The progress of the Wesleys' spiritual pilgrimages between February and May 1738 was directed by the counsel and teaching of Bohler and it climaxed at Pentecost that year. Charles Wesley found the assurance of sins forgiven on Pentecost Sunday while staying in a Moravian home in London. Three days later a similar experience of 'heart-warming' came to John while attending a Moravian gathering. His record of what happened that Wednesday evening in Aldersgate Street was couched in Moravian language. 'I felt my heart strangely warmed, and I felt I did trust in Christ, Christ alone, for salvation, and an assurance was given me....'[119]

The Wesley brothers and the Moravians worked together very closely in London and later in 1738 John Wesley visited the Moravian headquarters in Hernhuth in German and met the founder, Count Zinzendorf and other leaders. When his itinerant preaching ministry began in Bristol in April 1739, he had the full support of the Moravian brethren and his many letters to James Hutton, a leading English Moravian, shows how close this friendship was. Differences began to emerge when a German Moravian, Philip Molther, introduced 'Stillness' practices into the Fetter Lane Society. This teaching advocated that seekers after God should refrain from all the means of grace, including Scripture reading, prayer and hearing sermons, and wait for the Spirit to bring to them the gift of faith. The Wesleys

---

[118] J. Wesley, *Letters*, Vol. 1, p.351.
[119] J. Wesley, *Works [BE]*, Vol. 18, p.250.

opposed this emphasis, convinced that through these means of grace God mediated His Spirit to bring people to repentance and faith. There was a split in the Fetter Lane Society and a large number followed the Wesleys out of that Society and joined with them in a new fellowship, the first of the many Wesleyan Societies that would be organised in the years ahead. [120]

Although the Wesleys and the Moravians still shared some Love-feasts together, there was disagreement among them on the question of the believer's sanctification. With their strong Lutheran background, the Moravians emphasised the imputation of Christ's righteousness to the Christian. Increasingly the Wesleys, while advocating imputation, were also stressing the transforming work of the Spirit in the Christian's life and spoke of imparted or inherent righteousness as well. The Christian is not only accounted righteous but he is being made righteous. This emphasis convinced John Wesley that the Moravian teaching, unless it was expressed very carefully, opened the door to antinomianism. This dispute with old friends who esteemed each other highly might well have been amicably resolved but for the intervention of Count Zinzendorf. On a visit to London in 1741 he met with John Wesley and was totally unsympathetic to any notion of imparted holiness. James Hutton's biographer later recorded that Zinzendorf openly disparaged what he called the Wesleys' 'self-made holiness.' In his capacity as 'bishop and guardian of the Church of the Brethren,' he publicly branded John and Charles Wesley as 'false teachers and deceivers of souls' and declared that fellowship between the Moravians and Methodists could only be restored if the Wesleys dropped their delusions about 'Christian perfection.'[121]

---

[120] The Wesley brothers and their followers began to meet at the Foundery, a building which they purchased in the Moorfields district of London. The Foundery became the headquarters for the Wesleys' work for almost forty years. See *The Journal of the Rev. John Wesley*, edited by Nehemiah Curnock; 8 Vols: London: Epworth Press, 1938, Vol. 11, pp.316-319.

[121] D. Benham, *Memories of James Hutton*, London, 1856, p.112.

It was John Wesley's growing unhappiness about these divisions between the three groupings of the revival movement that led him to propose a conference of all the parties in an attempt to heal the breaches. He took the initiative to call the leaders together in London in August 1743. George Whitefield responded positively and Howell Harris likewise. Harris, a recognised leader of the revival work in Wales, was a close friend of both Whitefield and the Wesleys and a man of a truly catholic spirit. Although his theological persuasions put him closer to Whitefield than the Wesleys, both parties appreciated him with deep affection. Charles Wesley recorded that he was itinerating in Cornwall when John wrote and asked him to attend the conference. Whitefield, Harris and the Wesley brothers convened but the Moravians were not represented. John Wesley invited one of their leading preachers, August Spangenberg, an old friend of his from their days together in Georgia, but just before the conference was due to start, Spangenberg left England for America. This was a blow to John Wesley's high hopes that the gathering would resolve differences among brethren and bring about a closer co-operation in the work of evangelism and building up the work of God. The reason for the Moravians' refusal to take part is not certain but Arnold Dallimore makes a very reasonable assumption. He argues that at this time the Moravians were hoping to forge closer ties with the Church of England and made it clear that they would participate in the conference only if the Archbishop of Canterbury was also invited.

In his *Journal* for August 1743 he recorded that for some time he had a 'strong desire to unite with Mr Whitefield as far as possible, to cut off needless dispute.' He reasoned that the two sides were divided over three main points; unconditional election, irresistible grace and final perseverance. Attempting to heal the breach and reconcile estranged friends, Wesley proposed a modification in his own views. He would accept a doctrine of unconditional election for some, provided it did not entail the necessary damnation of all the rest. Nor would he object to an interpretation of irresistible grace, unless it implied that those on whom it worked without producing any response were therefore irrevocably damned. As to final perseverance, Wesley went even further in trying to effect a harmonious unity among the leaders of the revival. He confessed that he believed there was a state of grace from which the Christian could not fall away.[122]

On any scale of measurement Wesley's olive branch was a remarkable gesture. In the history of theological disputes among Christian theologians, there are few examples of those who were willing to surrender previously-held views for the sake of co-operation and brotherly affection. Far more often these disputes have led to protagonists hardening their attitudes, and, it is to be feared, also their hearts. John Wesley knew that many would interpret his proposals as a 'climb down' on his part, but there is no doubt that he genuinely wanted to be reconciled with Whitefield. He published this remarkable theological eirenicon in his *Journal* for all to see. Whether or not the two parties ever discussed it is uncertain but, sadly, nothing came from these proposals. John Wesley had taken considerable steps to bring old friends together and even though they failed, they were welcome examples of the catholic spirit.

Five years later Whitefield made an effort to re-unite the divided Methodists. He wrote to John Wesley in September 1748, saying that an 'external' union was not practical because he (Whitefield) was planning to spend most of his time in America and he did not intend to gather his followers in England into societies. He expressed his disappointment that their work had not allowed them to meet for some years and he asked Wesley to pray for him.[123] A year later the two groups planned a Conference in Bristol and Whitefield, John and Charles Wesley and Howell Harris attended. They attempted to discuss the common ground between them and agreed not to engage in argument and polemic. Perhaps by now both Whitefield and Wesley acknowledged that their publicised wrangling ten years earlier had had melancholy consequences. If both men had acted with less haste in vindicating their own positions, later hostilities might have been

---

[122] J. Wesley, *Journal*, Vol. 3, pp.84-86.
[123] J. Wesley, *Works [BE]*, Vol. 26, p.327
.

avoided. If only John Wesley had not gone to the printers with his trenchant sermon, *Free Grace*! And if only George Whitefield had directed his *Letter* to Wesley in private, rather than publishing it!

All of us who truly long for open, honest, heart-felt and Spirit-filled fellowship and co-operation among evangelicals in the 21st century, must learn from what happened in the 18th century. The catholic spirit certainly means that we will not attack and criticise one another openly, nor will we have any part in allowing unfounded rumours and innuendo to make us suspicious of one another. But the catholic spirit also means that, whatever convictions we hold personally on the questions of predestination, perfection theories, gifts of the Sprit, women in ministry, and such like, we will pray for, support and work with all those who believe and proclaim the great doctrines of historic orthodox Christianity.

By the late 1740s, John Wesley found himself taking care of a rapidly-growing number of people who had joined his Societies in their search for salvation. To help in this quest and confirm those already in the way of salvation, Wesley instituted class meetings, band meetings, Love-feasts, quarterly meetings and other such means of grace. Full-time travelling preachers were recruited, assistants and local leaders were appointed and the circuit system was set up. John Wesley also began to compose, extract from other works, edit and publish many writings for the instruction of his preachers and the edification of his people. These publications ranged from popular evangelistic tracts like, *A Word to a Swearer*, *A Word to a Drunkard*, to reasoned apologetics like, *An Appeal to Men of Reason and Religion*. In 1749 he began a very ambitious publishing project. This was his, *Christian Library, fifty duodecimo volumes, subtitled Extracts from and Abridgements of the Choicest Pieces of Practical Divinity which have been Published in the English Tongue*. Believing that 'reading Christians will be knowing Christians,'[124] he edited extracts that began in the 1st century with Clement of Rome and extended to works written in the 18th century.

---

[124] J. Wesley, *Letters*, Vol. 6, p.201.

Wesley concentrated on what he called 'practical divinity'; those writings that were meant to confirm the Christian faith and build up believers in holy living. In his own words, this *Christian Library* would constitute 'Christianity reduced to practice.'[125]

> I have endeavoured to extract such a collection of English Divinity, as (I believe), is all true, all agreeable to the oracles of God: as is all practical, unmixed with controversy of any kind; and all intelligible to plain men: such as is not superficial, but going down to the depth, and describing the height of Christianity. And yet not mystical, not obscure to any of those who are experienced in the ways of God.... I take no author for better, or worse; (as indeed I dare not call any man Rabbi) but endeavour to follow each so far as he follows Christ.[126]

A Christian Library, a huge literary undertaking for a busy, travelling preacher is a very good guide to John Wesley's understanding of both Christian truth and Christian practice. *A Christian Library* demonstrates how Wesley's hermeneutic, in a typical Anglican way, was constituted by scripture, tradition and reason. But there was a fourth dimension to this approach to Christian theology and practice – and that was experience. Wesley was sure that the 'experience' of sins forgiven and the indwelling Christ were privileges granted to Christians in every age. *A Christian Library* was intended not only as an instructor in Christian truth but also a means of confirming Christian practice and encouraging what Wesley often summarised as true Christian experience – the 'faith that works by love' (Gal. 5:6).

John Wesley's *A Christian Library* was yet another illustration of his deep commitment to the catholic spirit. When the contents of the *A Christian Library* are examined carefully, it gives a remarkable insight into the scope and depth of Wesley's Christian sympathies. The extract represents the Apostolic Fathers, continental authors, Anglican and Puritan writers and some anonymous devotional writings. The Fathers are represented by Clement of Rome, Polycarp, Ignatius and Macarius. Wesley's application of the 4th century Macarius is typical of his penchant for practical Christian instruction:

---

[125] J. Wesley, *A Christian Library*, 30 Vols., 1749-1755, Vol. 11, p.3.
[126] J. Wesley, *A Christian Library*, 30 Vols., 1749-1755, Vol. 11, p.3.

Whatever he insists upon essential, is durable, is necessary. What he continually labours to cultivate in himself and others is, the real life of God in the heart and soul, that kingdom of God, which consist in righteousness, and peace, and joy in the Holy Ghost. He is ever quickening and stirring up in his audience, endeavouring to kindle in them a steady zeal, an earnest desire, an inflamed ambition, to recover that Divine image we were made in; to be conformable to Christ our Head; to be daily sensible more and more.... [of] such a victorious faith as overcomes the world, and working by love, is ever fulfilling the whole law of God.[127]

If Wesley's inclusion of the writings of Macarius in his Christian Library does not provoke much surprise, it is different with the writings of two medieval Roman Catholic writers. They were Antoinette Bourignon (1616-1680), a Spanish Quietist, and Miguel de Molinos (1649-1697), also a Spanish Quietist. While John Wesley took a vigorous stand against Roman Catholic doctrines such as transubstantiation, purgatory, indulgences, papal infallibility and all forms of mariolatry, yet he was willing to recognise that some Catholic writers were helpful in promoting practical Christianity. Although he was later castigated by Richard Hill and Augustus Toplady for promoting popery, Wesley defended his use of these writers. Whatever the deficiencies in their understanding of some Christian doctrines, they had deep, personal acquaintance with Christ through his Spirit. Both were exponents of a kind of meditative spirituality that placed great emphasis on waiting on God, and little of what could be described as distinctive Roman dogma was found in their pages. Wesley also made it plain that when he selected an extract from any particular book, it did not mean that he agreed with everything else in that volume, much less what that author might have written elsewhere. In compiling the *A Christian Library*, Wesley made it plain that he was an editor, not the author. Wesley's attitude to these Catholic mystics is well summarised in the preface he wrote is his extensively-edited *Life* of Madam Guyon.

---

[127] J. Wesley, *A Christian Library*, Vol. 1, p.71. Patristic scholarship is now fairly unanimous that these *Homilies*, traditionally attributed to the 4th century Egyptian monk, Macarius were almost certainly written by a disciple of Gregory of Nyssa.

The following contains all that is scriptural and rational; all that tends to the genuine love of God and our neighbour. In the meantime, most of what to be contrary to Scripture and reason is omitted.... The grand source of all her mistakes was this: the not being guided by the written word. She did not take the Scriptures for the rule of her actions; at most it was but the secondary rule. Inward impressions, which she called inspirations, were her primary rule. The written word was not a lantern to her feet, a light in all her paths.... Yet with all this dross, how much pure gold is mixed! So God did wink at involuntary ignorance....[128]

There are excellent things in most of the Mystic writers. As almost all of them lived in the Romish Church, they were lights whom the gracious providence of God raised up to shine in a dark place.[129]

Given John Wesley's well-known predilection for Anglican authors, especially those of the Reformation period, 1660-1700, the inclusion of extracts from their writings would be expected in his *A Christian Library*.[130] And they are there, including Thomas Ken, Jeremy Taylor, Simon Patrick, William Cave, John Tillotson, William Beveridge and many more. But there are just as many Puritan authors represented in his *A Christian Library* and the list of names in impressive, including Richard Sibbes, Thomas Goodwin, Richard Alleine, Richard Baxter, Edmund Calamy, John Flavel, John Howe and others. Indications of the high esteem in which John Wesley held these and other Puritan writers can be found scattered throughout all his publications, and in *A Christian Library* he gives specific reasons for including them. He was not blind to what he believed to be both their literary and

---

[128] J. Wesley, *Works*, Vol. 14, pp.276-278.
[129] J. Wesley, *Works*, Vol. 13, p.25.
[130] In 1789 Wesley wrote of the strong Anglican influence which he grew in Epworth, and indeed remained with him throughout his life. 'From a child, I was taught to love and reverence the Scriptures, the oracles of God; and, next to these, to esteem the primitive Fathers, the writers of the first three centuries. Nest after the primitive church, I esteemed our own, the Church of England, as the most scriptural national Church. I esteemed our own, the Church of England, as the most scriptural Church in the world.' J. Wesley, *Works*, Vol. 13, p.272.

theological imperfections, but their practical value more than compensated for these weaknesses.

> They are exceeding verbose, and full of circumlocutions and repetitions. But I persuade myself, most of these defects barefooted in the following sheets.... But it should not be concealed, there are other blemishes in the greater part of the Puritan writers. They drag in controversy on every occasion, nay, without any occasion or pretence at all. Another is, that they generally give a low and imperfect view of sanctification or holiness.... But abundant recompense is made for all their blemishes, by the excellence which may be observed in them.... Their judgement is generally deep and strong, their sentiments just and clear, and their tracts on every head full and comprehensive.... More particularly they do indeed exalt Christ. They set him forth in all his offices.... And next to God himself, they honour his Word. They are men mighty in the Scriptures, equal to any of those who went before them, and far superior to most that have followed them.... They are continually tearing the very roots of Antinomianism.... But the peculiar excellency of these writers seems to be, the building us up in our most holy faith.[131]

Among the Puritan writers from whom Wesley extracted material for his *A Christian Library* were some whose high Calvinism he had little sympathy with. But here he followed the same principle as when he made extracts from medieval Catholic writers; an extract did not necessarily mean Wesley's agreement with other parts of the writing. In both these examples, Wesley was putting the catholic spirit into practice. If the writer exalted and, in particular, promoted practical holiness, then his or her attachment to doctrines not acceptable to Wesley was no bar to his using the 'good grain.' With references to the English Puritans, Wesley's use of the writings of John Owen clearly demonstrates that for him the catholic spirit took precedence over personal opinions. Owen was unquestionably the most dogmatic Calvinist of the English Puritans and his book, *The Death of Christ,* was the most extensively-argued presentation of the doctrine of limited atonement that could be found. He was, not unnaturally, a vigorous exponent of the doctrine of absolute predestination and did not shy

---

[131] J. Wesley, *A Christian Library*, Vol. 4, pp.106, 107.

away from the doctrine that consequently flows from it – reprobation. To John Wesley, any concept of the doctrine of reprobation was utterly irreconcilable with his understanding of the love of God. He vehemently rejected the doctrine of unconditional election because 'it necessarily implies unconditional reprobation. Find out any election which does not imply reprobation, and I will agree to it.'[132]

Although Owen was the acknowledged defender of high Calvinist doctrine, yet Wesley included extracts from Owen's writings in his *A Christian Library*. When he used the Catholic mystics, he carefully avoided any extracts that promoted Catholic doctrine or mysticism. Likewise with his use of Owen. From the many volumes of the Puritan's works, Wesley avoided all controversial matter, and selected what was calculated to glorify Christ and incite the Christian to holy living. He made use of four of Owen's publications. They were his, *Mortifications of Sin in Believers, Of Temptation*, *The Nature of the Person of Christ*, and, *God and Man, and Of Communion with God, Son and the Holy Ghost*. In these writings the Christian met with 'practical divinity.' Wesley could recommend these works of Owen to every Christian seeking instruction in scriptural truth and guidance on the holy life. Wesley's catholic spirit prompted him to include extracts from the writings of this magisterial Calvinist theologian, but extracts that carefully avoided what Wesley considered to be unhelpful, and often confusing, theological speculation.

Two more examples of John Wesley's catholic spirit are worth noting briefly. In 1749 he published, 'A Letter to a Roman Catholic.' It acknowledged that Protestants and Roman Catholics held many prejudices about each other but it was not opinions on either side, or a particular mode of worship, that made a man a true Christian. All those who call themselves Protestant but in practice are 'common swearers, drunkards, wholemongers, liars…. in a word, all who live in open sin,' are really heathens. The true Protestant worships God in spirit and truth, loves God and his neighbour and walks in holiness. Wesley then challenges his Roman Catholic reader. Can he find fault with this

---

[132] J. Wesley, *Works*, Vol. 10, p.211.

description of a Christian? Is he following Christ in like manner? Is his whole life a sacrifice to God and is he delivered from both outward and inner sin? This alone is 'the old religion, true, primitive Christianity.'[133]

Wesley then proceeded to offer a remarkable *eirenicon* of Christian good will to Roman Catholics:

> Are we not thus far agreed.... If God still loveth us, we ought also to love one another.... Let the points wherein we differ stand aside; here are enough wherein we agree, enough to be the ground of every Christian temper, and of every Christian action. O brethren, let us not fall out by the way! I hope to see you in heaven. And if I practise the religion above described, you dare not say I shall go to hell. Then if we cannot as yet think alike in all things, at least we may love alike. Herein we cannot possibly do amiss. For of one point none can doubt a moment. 'God is love, and he that dwelleth in love, dwelleth in God, and God in him.'[134]

John Wesley was seeking what common ground he could find between Roman Catholics and himself. He was making a very important distinction between Roman Catholic dogma, which he repudiated, and Roman Catholic people whom he loved for Christ's sake. Their dogmas were 'a heap of erroneous opinions delivered by tradition from the fathers.'[135] The true gospel of salvation by faith alone had effectively driven popery out of England and that gospel alone could keep it out.[136] Wesley openly declared that he 'detested and abhorred the fundamental doctrines of the Church of Rome,'[137] but his attitude to Roman Catholic people was one of good will, concern for the bodies and souls, and a ready acknowledgement and conduct that many of them gave indisputable evidence of being true Christians. Here again there is testimony of how John Wesley endeavoured to distinguish between opinions and true faith. He was as forthright as any 18th

---

[133] J. Wesley, *Works*, Vol. 10, p.85.
[134] J. Wesley, *Works*, Vol. 10, p.85.
[135] J. Wesley, *Works*, Vol. 6, p.199.
[136] J. Wesley, *Works [BE]*, Vol. 1, p.129.
[137] J. Wesley, *Works*, Vol. 1, p.456.

century English Protestant in espousing what he believed to be the numerous and dangerous errors of Roman Catholics, but his love for his neighbour warmly and genuinely embraced Roman Catholics. Throughout his ministry he strongly maintained that there is a very important distinction between essential Christian doctrine and personal opinions. There can be no compromise on vital doctrine but opinions are another matter. He spelt it out in a letter to John Newton in 1765. 'You have admirably well expressed what I mean by an opinion contradistinction from an essential doctrine. Whatever is "compatible with a love to Christ and a work of grace" I term an opinion.'[138]

Our final look at how John Wesley demonstrated the true catholic spirit is concerned with his hopes for a practical working unity among England's evangelical clergy. Following a friendly meeting in March 1761 with Henry Venn, Vicar of Huddersfield, Wesley took positive steps towards bringing about a fraternal union among evangelical ministers. Writing to George Downing, an Essex rector, he spoke about how he had laboured for many years 'to unite, not scatter, the messengers of God.' Now he voiced the hope that all those who embraced essential Christian doctrines might come together in the kind of harmonious unity that would greatly enhance the work of God.

> I think it a great pity that the few clergymen in England who preach the three grand scriptural doctrines - Original Sin, Justification by Faith, and Holiness consequent thereon - should have any jealousies or misunderstandings between them. What advantage must this give to the common enemy! What a hindrance is it to the great work wherein they all are engaged! How desirable is it that there should be the most open, avowed intercourse between them![139]

Three years later John Wesley took this plan for unity among the evangelical clergy a step further. He wrote a letter to among fifty of the evangelical clergy in the Church of England, including George Whitefield, William Romaine, John Newton, Walter Shirley, Henry Venn and John Berridge. The plea, a coming together of all those who

---

[138] J. Wesley, *Letters*, Vol. 4, p.297.
[139] J. Wesley, *Letters*, Vol. 4, p.146.

were 'fellow labourers in His gospel.' Wesley reasoned: 'Ought not those who are united to one common Head, and employed by Him in one common work, be united to each other?' After naming those he wished to unite, Wesley added that this proposal included any other clergy who agreed on the doctrines of original sin, justification by faith and holiness of heart and life.[140]

Wesley then set out the kind of union he had in mind. It was not a unity of opinions, or expression or outward order; rather a unity of good will and mutual support. Hindrances would be removed when ministers did not judge or envy each other, were not displeased with others who had greater success than they had, and did not gossip about the faults, mistakes and infirmities of their brethren. But Wesley was concerned that this evangelical fraternity would be marked, not only by its avoidance of critical attitudes, but positively by the way it manifested the fruits of the Spirit. These brethren would love, think of and honour each other. They would speak respectfully of one another, defend each other's characters and help one another in every possible way. It would require an earnest effort on the part of all concerned to desire this unity, and it would require the grace and power of God working through them to accomplish it.

> All nature is against it, every wrong temper and fashion; love of honour and praise, of power, of pre-eminence; anger, resentment, pride, long-contracted habit, and prejudice lurking in ten thousand forms. The devil and all his angels are against it.... All the world, all that know not God, are against it.... But surely 'with God all things are possible.'[141]

John Wesley was deeply disappointed that most of the clergy to whom he wrote did not even bother to reply to him. Just as he had done in early years in trying to bring the Methodist and Moravian preacher together, now he was attempting to unite the evangelical clergy in the Church of England. He longed for a unity of purpose and vision among his brethren that would strengthen their united efforts in evangelism

---

[140] J. Wesley, *Works [BE]*, Vol. 21, p.456.
[141] J. Wesley, *Works [BE]*, Vol. 21, pp.457, 458.

and in building up the work of God. His vision and hope and prayer was that the catholic spirit might characterise all those who truly loved God and their neighbours. As he repeatedly said: 'If we cannot think alike, than at least let us love alike.' If that catholic spirit was needed among the people of God in Britain in the 18th century, it is needed no less in this 21st century. And it is fitting that this attempt to demonstrate what John Wesley meant by the catholic spirit should conclude with words by his brother Charles, words expressing that what unites us in Christ is far more important than our denominational labels or our theologian slogans.

> Sweetly now we all agree
> Touched with softest sympathy
> Kindly for each other care
> Every member feel its share.
>
> Love, like death, hath all destroyed
> Tendered all distinctions void
> Names and sects, and parties fall
> Thou, O Christ, are all in all. [142]

---

[142] G. Osborn, Ed. *The Poetical Works of John and Charles Wesley*, 13 Vols. London, 1868-1872, Vol. 1. p.362.

Selected Bibliography

John Wesley: The Supremacy of Grace

James Orr, *The Progress of Dogma*, Glasgow, 1897.

John Wesley, *The Works of John Wesley,* 14 Vols. Nazarene Publishing House, Kansas City, Missouri, 1955.

The Bicentennial Edition of the Works of John Wesley, 20 Vols. Abingdon Press, Nashville, 1989-2016.

The Letters of the Rev. John Wesley, 8 Vols. Edited by John Telford, Epworth Press, London, 1931.

The Journal of the Rev. John Wesley, 8 Vols. Edited by Nehemiah Curnock, Epworth Press, London, 1938.

John Wesley, *Explanatory Notes upon The New Testament*, London, 1754.

John Wesley, *A Christian Library: Consisting of Extracts from and Abridgements of the Choicest Pieces of Practical Divinity,* 30 Vols. London, 1818.

A.S. Wood, *The Burning Heart: John Wesley, Evangelist,* Exeter, 1967.

Scriptual Holiness: The Methodist Distinctive

Paul M. Bassett, *Exploring Christian Holiness,* Vol. 2, pp.164-177, Nazarene Publishing House, Kansas City, 1974.

H.R. Dunning, *Grace, Faith and Holiness,* Nazarene Publishing House, Kansas City, 1988.

R.N. Flew, *The Idea of Perfection in Christian Theology,* Epworth Press, 1972.

A.E. McGrath, *Christian Theology,* Inter-Varsity Press, 1994. *Justification by Faith,* Inter-Varsity Press, 1988.

The Flame, Vol. 1, No. 1, April-May, 1935.

Harald Lindstrom, *Wesley and Sanctification*, Epworth Press, 1950.

Maynard James, *Evangelise*, Burnley, Lancashire, 1945.

Thomas C. Oden, *John Wesley's Scriptural Christianity,* Zondervan Publishing House, 1994.

G. Osborn, *The Poetical Works of John and Charles Wesley*, 13 Vols., Editor, G. Osborn, Wesleyan Methodist Conference Office, 1869.

W.E. Sangster, *The Path to Perfection*, Epworth Press, 1943.

Tyerman, *The Life and Times of the Rev. John Wesley*, Vol. 2, Hodder and Stoughton, London, 1873.

John Wesley, *The Letters of John Wesley,* Edited by John Telford, 8 Vols., Epworth Press, London, 1931.

John Wesley, *The Journal of the Rev. John Wesley*, 8 Vols. Edited by Nehemiah Curnock, Epworth Press, London, 1938.

John Wesley, *The Bicentennial Edition of John Wesley*, 20 Vols. Abingdon Press, Nashville, 1989-2016.

C. Urquhart, *Holy Fire*, Monarch Books, 1984.

John Wesley: Protagonist of the Catholic Spirit

D. Benham, *Memories of James Hutton*, London, 1856.

John Wesley, *The Works of John Wesley,* 14 Vols. Nazarene Publishing House, Kansas City, Missouri, 1955.

The Bicentennial Edition of the Works of John Wesley, 20 Vols. Abingdon Press, Nashville, 1989-2016.

The Letters of the Rev. John Wesley, 8 Vols. Edited by John Telford, Epworth Press, London, 1931.

The Journal of the Rev. John Wesley, 8 Vols. Edited by Nehemiah Curnock, Epworth Press, London, 1938.

John Wesley, *A Christian Library: Consisting of Extracts from and Abridgements of the Choicest Pieces of Practical Divinity,* 30 Vols. London, 1819.

Books by Revd Dr Herbert Boyd McGonigle

William Cooke on Entire Sanctification, Beacon Hill Press, Kansas City, Missouri, 1978.

The Arminianism of John Wesley, Moorleys Print & Publishing, Ilkeston, Derbyshire, 1988.

John Wesley and the Moravians, Moorleys Print & Publishing, Ilkeston, Derbyshire, 1995.

John Wesley's Doctrine of Prevenient Grace, Moorleys Print & Publishing, Ilkeston, Derbyshire, 1995.

Scriptural Holiness: The Wesleyan Distinctive, Moorleys Print & Publishing, Ilkeston, Derbyshire, 1995.

Sufficient Saving Grace: John Wesley's Evangelical Arminianism, 350 pages, Paternoster Publishing, Carlisle, Cumbria, 2001.

To God Be The Glory: The Killadeas Convention 1952-2002, Moorleys Print & Publishing, Ilkeston, Derbyshire, 2002.

John Wesley's Arminian Theology: An Introduction, Moorleys Print & Publishing, Ilkeston, Derbyshire, 2005.

A Burning and a Shining Light: The Life and Ministry of William Bramwell, Moorleys Print & Publishing, Ilkeston, Derbyshire, 2009.

Christianity or Deism? John Wesley's Response to John Taylor's Denial of the Doctrine of Original Sin, Moorleys Print & Publishing, Ilkeston, Derbyshire, 2012.

John Wesley: Exemplar of the Catholic Spirit, Moorleys Print & Publishing, Ilkeston, Derbyshire, 2014.

Charles Wesley: For All, For All My Saviour Died, Moorleys Print & Publishing, Ilkeston, Derbyshire, 2014.

John Wesley: The Death of Christ, Moorleys Print & Publishing, Ilkeston, Derbyshire, 2014.

Epworth: The Cradle of Methodism, Moorleys Print & Publishing, Ilkeston, Derbyshire, 2014.

John Wesley: Doctrine of Final Judgement, Moorleys Print & Publishing, Ilkeston, Derbyshire, 2015.

Thomas Walsh: Saint and Scholar, Moorleys Print & Publishing, Ilkeston, Derbyshire, 2015.

Our Story: Autobiographical thoughts from the pen of Revd. Dr. Herbert B. McGonigle, Nazarene Theological College Archives, Manchester, 2015.

Dr. Adam Clarke: Methodist Preacher and Scholar, Moorleys Print & Publishing, Ilkeston, Derbyshire, 2015.

Gideon Ouseley: Methodist Preacher and Biblical Scholar, Moorleys Print & Publishing, Ilkeston, Derbyshire, 2015.

Thomas Cook: Evangelist and Saint, Moorleys Print & Publishing, Ilkeston, Derbyshire, 2016.

The Methodist Pentecost, 1758-1763, Moorleys Print & Publishing, Ilkeston, Derbyshire, 2016.

John Fletcher, Methodist Saint and Scholar, Moorleys Print & Publishing, Ilkeston, Derbyshire, 2016.

An Appreciation of Revd. Dr. John Henry Jowett's Heaven's Hallelujah, Moorleys Print & Publishing, Ilkeston, Derbyshire, 2016.

General William Booth, Moorleys Print & Publishing, Ilkeston, Derbyshire, 2016.